500

sushi

500
sushi

the only sushi compendium you'll ever need

Caroline Bennett
with Hong Sui Li & Sami Nkaili

SELLERS
PUBLISHING

A Quintet Book

Published by Sellers Publishing, Inc.
161 John Roberts Road, South Portland, Maine 04106
Visit our Web site: www.sellerspublishing.com
E-mail: rsp@rsvp.com

Copyright © 2013 Quintet Publishing Limited.
All rights reserved. No part of this publication may be reproduced, stored in a retrieval system, or transmitted in any form or by any means, electronic, mechanical, photocopying, recording, or otherwise, without the written permission of the copyright holder.

ISBN: 978-1-4162-0881-5
e-ISBN: 978-1-4162-0900-3
Library of Congress Control Number: 2012942541
QTT.FSUS

This book was conceived, designed, and produced by
Quintet Publishing Limited
6 Blundell Street
London N7 9BH
United Kingdom

Chefs/Food Stylists: Hong Sui Li and Sami Nkaili
Photographer: Ian Garlick
Art Director: Michael Charles
Project Editor: Ross Fulton
Editorial Director: Donna Gregory
Publisher: Mark Searle

10 9 8 7 6 5 4 3 2 1

Printed in China by 1010 Printing International Ltd.

contents

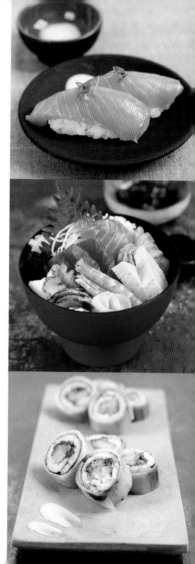

introduction

Say "Japanese food" to almost anyone and the chances are they will say "sushi." From Seoul to New York via Munich and Madrid, it is Japan's most famous culinary export. Perhaps this is because sushi is synonymous with the traditions and culture of Japan in so many ways. Japan is an island country surrounded by seas that are abundant with a huge variety of fish. Its land mass is relatively small, and much of that is given over to rice cultivation; the steep slopes of the Japanese Alps don't allow for large arable stretches of land. Thus a national dish based on the nutrition available in fish and rice was inevitable. As well, from an aesthetic point of view, sushi is the embodiment of Zen principles of minimalism, reflecting on nature's harmony and balance.

We usually rely very heavily on our sense of smell, more so even than our sense of taste, to appreciate food. Sushi, being cold, has very little aroma, so we must rely wholly upon our taste buds being stimulated by just the sushi's presentation.

The essence of Japanese aesthetics is embodied in the ideal of wabi sabi, which seeks to appreciate the whole of something being greater than the sum of its parts. Wabi sabi is a state of consciousness. It involves cultivating an awareness of your own aesthetic experience of a material object, and enjoying its specific and often hidden beauty. Eating sushi is about various different aspects of appreciation, from being delighted by the eye, intrigued by the texture, or captured by the lingering taste of the fresh, energizing nature of the sea.

A succcessful sushi dish makes a very distinct impression without any one aspect or flavor emerging as dominant or obvious. It is an art form and is considered an extension of nature in Japan, where food is so fresh that it tastes of the ingredients themselves rather what has

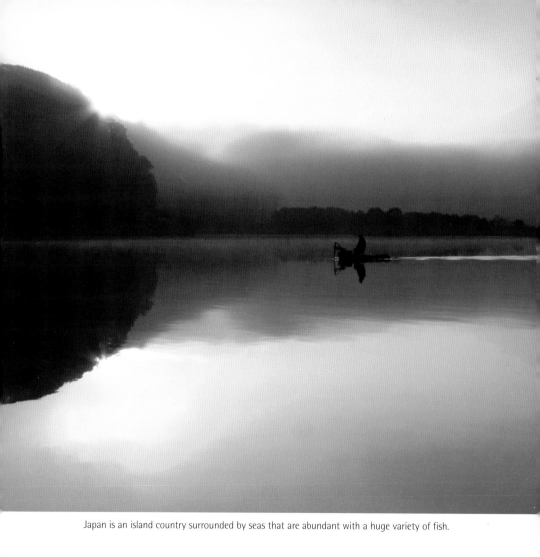

Japan is an island country surrounded by seas that are abundant with a huge variety of fish.

Delicate red mullet sashimi provides subtle and complex tastes and textures (page 190).

been done to them. Ingredients are introduced in varying degrees of rawness, nothing is overcooked; one feels close to food in its natural state.

Developing an understanding of the integrity of the raw ingredients requires patience and skill, and thus a sushi chef in Japan will toil away cleaning the display fridge or fish tank or floor for the first few years of his apprenticeship, before being allowed to enter behind the sushi counter.

In a traditional sushi bar in Japan, one is seated in front of the sushi master, where he will deftly slice and meld the sushi in front of you. With speed and precision that comes from many years of training, he produces a couple of neat oblong-shaped nigiri with all the grains of rice, it is said, facing in the same direction. In this traditional environment the reverence that Japan holds for its food is illustrated in the relationship between diner and sushi master, where a quality of mutual trust and appreciation between the two is struck. The sushi master is, after all, preparing raw fish, which in the hands of an inexperienced chef could have undesirable consequences.

Sushi wasn't always this uplifting, though, as originally it was nothing more than a means of preserving fish for the inclement winter months, when fishing was dangerous. Rice was packed around the fish fillets and left to ferment, then discarded before the aging fish flesh was eaten.

Gradually, over centuries, this style of sushi became oshi zushi or pressed sushi, where layers of fish and rice are pressed down. This style is still found today (see pages 265 and 266), but the more commonly known nigiri-style sushi today is from Tokyo, and was introduced in the early 1800s. There is no fermenting, no pressing into molds, no waiting. Thus sushi became the world's first "fast food."

sushi etiquette

To describe sushi as "parcels of vinegared rice with various toppings of usually fish or shellfish" does little to reveal its cultural subtleties and complexities. But a trip to a traditional sushi bar uncovers a lot more. You will enter a sushi bar through the traditional noren curtain. In days gone by, a dirty one used to signify a popular sushi bar, as it was customary to wipe your hands on the curtain as you left!

Once inside, you will be greeted with a welcoming "Irrashaimase" from the sushi chefs standing behind the immaculate white cypress sushi counter. The sushi counter is the place to sit to soak up the atmosphere and be treated to the day's selection of best fish. You will be offered a wet towel, or oshibori, and a cup of hot sencha green tea, which is called agari rather than ocha in a sushi bar. The sushi master will lean over and put down a small dish of gari ginger pickle to refresh your palate between each sushi. It is considered unseemly to eat this all at once as one might a salad or garnish. Now you are settled in, you are ready to order.

Some like to start with slices of sashimi; others might want to dive straight into the sushi. Generally, one starts with nigiri sushi (pages 56–91), and in Japan these make up most of the sushi dinner, before moving on to gunkan (pages 92–121), and lastly maki or temaki sushi (pages 122–187, 220–245).

In the West, we tend to reverse this, preferring the more flamboyant flavors of a futomaki to the reserved ones of a nigiri. In any event, start with subtle, delicate whitefish, such as bream or snapper, before moving on to fattier fish such as salmon and tuna, or "shiny" fish as they are called in Japan, like mackerel and herring.

Cooked seafood such as shrimp or octopus are eaten toward the end of the nigiri selection. You will probably finish your sushi dinner with rolled sushi, and the chef might ask you whether you'd like it cut into 6 or 8 maki pieces or as a temaki hand roll.

It is commonplace not to order in a sushi bar, rather relying on the chef to size you up, and determine a suitable sushi course for you. Omakase dining (leave it up to the chef) is a wonderful way to enjoy sushi, but be warned — it is invariably not the cheapest. Refresh your palate with the gari ginger in between each type of sushi, especially after an oily fish such as mackerel, so as to cleanse the palate for your next morsel.

Be aware when you order at a sushi counter that nigiri and gunkan are always served in pairs, while hosomaki and futomaki come as whole rolls of six or eight pieces. Try to eat each nigiri and gunkan in one whole mouthful, as biting them in bits is not elegant.

Fill your soy sauce bowl with only enough to cover the bottom of the bowl. It is not good etiquette to fill it to the brim. It is considered courteous to pour the soy sauce for your guest. If you are eating both sushi and sashimi, you should have two bowls, one for your sashimi where you might want to add a small dab of wasabi to the bowl and mix it into the soy sauce. Or you can dab a little wasabi directly on the sashimi slices and dip gently into the soy sauce. The other bowl is for your sushi because it is not a good practice to add wasabi to your soy. The chef will already have seasoned the sushi with wasabi. Be aware it may even be considered insulting to add more wasabi to your sushi master's creations!

Deftly pick up the sushi and place it fish- or topping-side down into the soy, lightly dipping it rather than soaking it. If you place it rice-side down, the rice ball will fall apart and any subtle flavor is lost.

It is perfectly acceptable to not use chopsticks to eat sushi. Indeed, the more high-class or traditional the sushi bar, the more likely you are to eat sushi with your hands. There is something poignant about being handed sushi directly from a chef's masterful hands; using chopsticks puts a distance between you and your sushi master and breaks the spell.

Chopsticks are essential to eat just about everything else though, so it is best to get to grips with them to eat the sashimi, the pickles, and the miso soup or any accompanying hot dishes. The best advice I can give for chopsticks is to hold them gently; gripping them seems to make maneuvering virtually impossible. When you are not eating with them, place the pointed ends that hold the food onto the chopstick rest, or if one isn't given, then rest them on the soy bowl. Never lick or suck your chopsticks.

Never stand them vertically in a bowl of rice or transfer food from your chopsticks to another's; both of these actions are more appropriate in some religious rituals than at the dinner table. Never use your own chopsticks in a shared plate of food; either use the serving chopsticks or if there are none, turn your chopsticks around the other way to serve yourself.

Miso soup or suimono clear soup usually come toward the end of the sushi dinner, and signifies that the diner is replete. Miso soup is never drunk as an appetizer in Japan.

a plea for our oceans

I find this section the hardest to write. When I started on my sushi journey, I knew little about the plight of our oceans, but now that I am aware of the destruction our global fishing industry has wreaked on our seas, I feel a real sadness for our waters and the beautiful creatures that live in them.

We are hugely reliant on the health of our seas; they absorb carbon for us, create temperate weather patterns, present a myriad of medical solutions, and above all provide much of the world with its main source of protein and good nutrition. And yet, like so many other things in life, we turn a blind eye to the devastation we have inflicted on nature. No less than 80 percent of fish stocks are fished to the maximum allowable level or are overfished. That leaves only 20 percent doing okay. We have a duty to care for the next generation and, indeed, to preserve the few resources that we have left.

I firmly believe that we can find a solution to the problems of our seas with a little help from Japanese philosophy. There is as much good as there is bad in the world, as much yin as there is yang, but our complicity or inertia can lead to the bad overriding the good. Instead, we need to play an active role in our choices. There is nothing more grounding and compassionate than the choices we make about what we eat.

Our collective choices can change the whole way we take fish from the seas. Changing habits of a lifetime doesn't happen overnight, though, so accept that change in the world's fishing industries will take a while. These days it is not hard to go online and find wonderful words of wisdom from Slow Food, Monterey Bay Aquarium, Greenpeace, and the Marine Stewardship Council to name but a few. I urge you to get to know how your fish was caught; if we catch plentiful fish unsustainably, then they won't be sustainable for long.

The last word goes to Carlo Petrini, founder of the groundbreaking organization Slow Food, and to whom I am most grateful for inspiring change in me: Anyone who thinks of themselves as a food lover but does not have any environmental awareness is naïve — whereas an ecologist who does not enjoy the pleasures of food certainly has a sadder life.

japanese knives

It is said that the sushi master's knife is as precious to him as the sword is to a samurai. The yanagiba, long and narrow and pointed at the end, are often described as sashimi knives. Sushi chefs never share their yanagiba, and this is because it becomes an extension of their arm, finely tuned to be able to expertly slice and cut to the rhythm of their art.

A sushi chef will keep his yanagiba knife exceptionally sharp so as to maximize the flavor, texture, and appearance of the fish. It is up to you which grade of knife you wish to use, but bear in mind that while the very expensive stainless steel knife keeps its sharpness well, it doesn't take well to the sharpening stone.

A sushi chef regularly sharpens his knife on sharpening stones (never a steel knife sharpener or an electric one) that vary in coarseness depending on the age and quality of the knife. When not in use, the knives should be wrapped in a clean, dry cloth.

If they are not to be used for a while, it is best to rub a little vegetable oil over the blade to prevent rusting. Japanese yanagiba knives differ from Western knives in that they are flat on one side. This enables the knife to slice through the fish flesh without causing the flesh to fray, leaving the flesh looking translucent and iridescent. True to so many things in Japan, the simplicity belies the complexity and the many other benefits of good cutting techniques.

The texture is one such very important feature. Westerners who say they don't like sushi or sashimi, never say that it doesn't taste good. Rather, it is the texture they cannot stand — the very feel of the food. The Japanese appreciate texture almost as much as they appreciate taste, so the contrast of warm, pliable grains of rice under a slice of cool, resilient fish exemplifies the unwritten rule of opposites being complementary. Last, the knives, like so many other elements in the making of sushi, play a key role in reducing the buildup of bacteria on the fish flesh. A well-kept knife produces cleaner, safer sushi as it reduces the surface area exposed to oxidization.

Sake is the traditional Japanese rice wine that can be enjoyed, warm or cold, with sushi.

choosing and filleting fish

Look out for these signs when choosing your fish: The gills should be bright red, the eyes translucent and bright, the skin firm so that when you press a finger on the flesh it doesn't leave an indentation. It should be slimy to the touch, and it should smell of the sweetness of the sea and not at all fishy. If it does smell fishy, the fish's own enzymes have started to work on breaking down its flesh, and it is a sign that the fish is probably not palatable for eating raw. Don't forget to wash your hands before filleting fish to reduce the chance of a bacterial buildup.

sanmai oroshi 3-piece filleting round fish
Filleting in Japan is named after the number of pieces a fish is to be cut into, so for example, a sea bass is sanmai oroshi, or filleting into three.

Remove the scales with a sharp knife or scaler. You might find it handy to place the fish in a large plastic bag while you are doing this so as to not get fish scales scattered around your kitchen. Cut along under the gills where the head joins the body and remove the head. Cut open the stomach and remove the entrails, then clean out the dark red blood that is around the backbone area with a brush.

Wash the fish thoroughly. Place the fish on the chopping board and insert the knife into the back as far as the backbone and cut along the length of the fish from the head to the tail. Then turn the fish and insert the knife in the same fashion on the stomach side and remove the upper fillet. Do the same on the other side, first cutting in toward the backbone, then removing the second fillet from the stomach cut. The fish will now be in three pieces: two fillets and a backbone.

Remove the stomach bones from the two fillets by holding your knife horizontally and slicing them out of the fillets. Now cut each fillet into two along the line of the missing backbone. Last, cut off the parts with the tiny bones next to the cut you have just made. To remove the skin, place the fillets skin-side facing down on your board, gently insert the knife at the tail end between the skin and the flesh, and raise the blade slightly. Holding the tail end firmly in place with your left hand, run the blade along the bottom of the fish, cutting away the skin as thinly as possible.

As a general observation, always try to fillet while moving the knife in one long, sweeping motion, rather than hacking away. A cleanly cut fish improves the appearance of the sashimi, it enhances the texture on the palate, and importantly, it reduces the oxidization of a jagged-edged flesh, which in turn prevents the flesh from deteriorating and the buildup of bacteria, very important considerations when eating fish raw.

squid & cuttlefish

You must make sure to use freshly caught squid as it will be eaten raw. It is best to use frozen squid if your fishmonger can't guarantee the freshness of the whole squid. If you are using a whole squid, place it on a chopping board. Holding the head in one hand, grasp the tentacles at their base and gently straighten them out with the other hand. Reach inside the body cavity and remove the translucent quill. Throw away the guts, trying not to pierce the ink sac, which can be retained if you'd like to use it.

Insert a knife into the body and carefully slit it down one side. Put a finger under the fin to separate it, and then pull off the fin and remove the thin membrane. Trim to remove the "wings" that can be seen attached to the body. Cut away the tentacles just in front of the eyes and squeeze out the small beak. Rinse and pat dry. For cuttlefish, follow the same steps as for squid, but cut the head on the cuttle side, open and remove the guts. The ink sac is attached to the other side.

gomai oroshi — 5-piece filleting for flat fish

This filleting technique is used mostly on large flat fish and, if you are less confident, on smaller flat fish, too, because it is easier to split the fillets than try to remove them in one piece. There are no scales to remove on a flat fish. Now follow the steps for 3-piece filleting, cutting the boneless side of the fillet into two, creating four boneless fillets, with the fifth piece being the central skeleton.

To do this, place the fish belly down on the cutting board, and cut along the curve of the outer fins on both sides, then cut through the center from tail to head. Pull the fillets off, starting at the center of the head end, the firmest part, and pull the fish away from the bone. Do the same on the other side. Turn the fish over and repeat on the belly side.

Cutting at an angle, remove the stomach lining and pull out any small bones with tweezers. Skin the fillets the same way as described in 3-piece filleting.

preparing large fish for neta slices

Large fish such as tuna and hamachi yellowtail, and often salmon, are characterized by a fattier, more tender texture, and so are somewhat unsatisfying if cut into thin slices. Each slice should be cut into pieces 3–4 inches long and 1 inch wide. Each slice should weigh around 3/4 ounce. Cut at right angles to the sinews; if the fish is cut in parallel slices, some pieces may turn out white and hard.

The best tuna is a prized ingredient in Japanese cuisine — Marinated Tuna Nigiri (page 58).

nigiri sushi technique

While fish plays the starring role in sushi, it would be nothing without the supporting role of the rice. Indeed, the rice makes all the difference to the texture and enjoyment of the small morsel of fish on the palate. It is important that the rice is evenly flavored and textured, and that the warmth of the rice ball complements the coolness of the fish. There is little worse than cold, compact rice on your sushi.

To make a perfect nigiri, try first to relax! Add about 2 tablespoons of vinegar to a small bowl of water. Wet your fingers and the palm of your left hand in it to help prevent the rice from sticking to your fingers and also to help sanitize them.

Place the neta (the generic term for any topping on a nigiri sushi) slice in your left hand. Lightly grip the end of the slice between your index finger and thumb, letting the slice rest lightly on the middle joints of your fingers. Now take a small ball of shari rice weighing about 1/2 ounce in your right hand and gently mold it to form the classic nigiri shape. While cupping the shari rice loosely in the palm of your right hand, take some wasabi with the index finger of the right hand and smear it gently on the center of the neta slice.

Place the shari rice ball on top of the neta slice. Gently curve the palm of your left hand, press firmly with the thumb of the same hand in the middle of the ball of rice to make an indentation. This ensures that the outside of the nigiri is firm while the inside remains sufficiently soft.

Roll the sushi down your left hand so it rests across the fingers of the left hand with the neta slice facing upward. Press the end of the shari rice with your left thumb, then rotate 180 degrees to press gently on the other end.

Extend your right index finger and middle finger over the top of the neta slice, but without pressing down with this hand, shape the sushi using the left hand, pressing upward. Pinch both sides of the sushi between your right middle finger and thumb to shape, then rotate the sushi 180 degrees.

The finished nigiri shape should be even and, if you've managed to handle the shari and neta as little as possible, the nigiri should look as though it were about to swim off!

Smoked fish is a non-traditional but delicious addition to nigiri — Tea-Smoked Salmon Nigiri (page 64).

maki rolling technique: futomaki

This same basic technique is used for both futomaki (thick rolls) and hosomaki (thin rolls). For futomaki one must be particularly careful in order to prevent the rice from bursting out of the nori and the fillings being crushed. Place a bowl of vinegared water at one side of your board. Place the nori, shiny side down, on top of a maki rolling mat, with the longer edge nearest yourself. Lay plastic wrap on your mat if you like.

Dip your fingers in the vinegared water and spread about 1/2 cup of shari rice evenly over the nori, making sure you leave a 3/4-inch gap of bare nori at the top (far side). Smear a dab of wasabi in the middle across the width of the roll. The amount would be to your taste. It's up to you now how you choose the fillings; always bear in mind the appearance and color balance of the finished maki.

Now for the tricky part! Press lightly on the middle of the roll with your index and middle finger and pick up the side of the maki mat closest to you with your thumbs.

In one fluid motion, roll the maki mat
forward, enclosing the fillings but leaving
the bare nori strip. Using your fingertips,
bring the mat down to meet the bare strip
of nori, to make sure the roll is sealed
properly. Press on the sides of the mat to
shape into a gentle square, then roll over
90 degrees and press again to shape.

Remove the mat, place it over the roll, and
press down once more to shape the edges.

Cut into 6 or 8 pieces, using a sharp, clean
knife dipped into a little water, pushing the
pieces away from you as you cut.

maki rolling technique: uramaki

These are like futomaki rolls but are rolled in reverse so that the nori is on the inside and the outer layer is open to any number of different ingredients. It is a highly decorative way of making sushi and appeals to Westerners.

Place a bowl of vinegared water at one side. Cover the bamboo maki mat with plastic wrap on both sides. Lay the sheet of nori on the plastic-covered mat with the long side facing you. Spread 1/2 cup of shari rice evenly over the nori, covering it right up to the edges. Spread evenly on top of the rice whatever ingredient you choose to use on the outside of your roll. Fish roes such as tobiko are popular choices, and you can also use micro greens such as shiso cress or mustard and cress.

Deftly pick up the nori at the corners and flip it over so that the nori is now face up. Arrange the fillings along the center of the nori. With your hands held over the base of the mat and pressing the mat down over the ingredients with your fingers as you go, roll the mat over the ingredients, leaving a 1-inch piece of nori visible at the top.

Press gently to mold the roll together. Lift up the mat, roll back a little, then roll forward to join the nori edges. Use gentle pressure to firm and mold the roll in the shape you like — square, oval, or round. Unfurl the mat and, if desired, evenly spread a topping around the roll's outer side.

Using a sharp knife, cut into 8 pieces by cutting the roll in half, then each half in halves again. Then cut the 4 quarters one more time to make 8 even pieces. Alternatively, you can cut the roll into 6 pieces. Cut gently so as to maintain your chosen shape.

basic recipes

Soy sauce, miso, mirin, rice vinegar, and dashi are

the main components of Japanese cuisine.

Familiarize yourself with these elegantly simple

components in their most widely used contexts, and

you will become confident enough to experiment.

tsuma — sashimi decoration

see variations page 46

Sashimi, raw fish served without rice, is never served solo. An unadorned slice of raw fish on a plate with nothing else is like eating bread without butter. Shredded vegetables such as daikon white radish and seaweeds are typically placed under, to the side, or sometimes as a garnish on top of the sashimi. The generic name for these garnishes is tsuma. Their purpose is not merely decorative, as they help cover up the smell of raw fish and provide some help with sterilizing, while others aid digestion. They also add to the color, texture, and scent of a dish. Once again, we see the harmony of beauty to the eye being beneficial to the body, and in adding vegetables to fish, the balance of nature.

1 tsp. of dried wakame seaweed
14-in. long piece of daikon white radish

Soak the seaweed in a little water for a few minutes. Drain and squeeze out the water. With a 6-in. long sharp knife, hold the daikon firmly against the knife, and rotate the daikon gradually to produce one long uniform strip.

Fold the strip into thirds, and cut into fine shreds. Plunge into ice water for at least 15 minutes. Drain the daikon and mix with the wakame. Make a bed of wakame and daikon tsuma and arrange your sashimi slices on top.

Serves 2

shari sushi rice

see variations page 47

Choosing a good rice is important in sushi; it must, once cooked, have optimal
absorbency qualities to ensure that the flavor of each rice grain is even and has a
consistently soft and sticky texture. Use short grain japonica white rice, which can be
found in all Japanese stores and health food shops, or arborio, Italian risotto rice.

2 cups short grain japonica rice   1 oz. sugar
2 1/4 cups water   1 tsp. salt
2 1/2 fl. oz. rice vinegar

Place the rice in a bowl and cover with cold water. Stir the water and the rice to allow the
impurities and outer bran layers to be washed away. Gently rub the rice with the base of
your palms to strip the rice of its outer layers. Discard the milky water. Repeat this process a
number of times until the water runs clear. Put the draining rice into a sieve to stand for
about 30 minutes. Put the rice and water into a rice cooker and cook for 10–15 minutes.
Alternatively, place the rice and water in a heavy-bottomed saucepan, and cover tightly with
a lid. Bring to a boil on medium heat and boil for 2–3 minutes. Reduce the heat to its lowest
setting and simmer for a further 10–12 minutes. Resist the temptation to lift the lid!

Once cooked, leave in the rice cooker or remove the saucepan from the heat, and let stand
without lifting the lid for an additional 15–20 minutes. Thoroughly mix the vinegar, sugar,
and salt together in a saucepan and heat gently over a low flame until the sugar and salt are
dissolved. Remove from the heat and let cool. Pour water into the wooden rice tub and leave
to absorb. Tip out the water and wipe with a dry dishcloth. Place the cooked rice in the pre-
soaked wooden rice tub or in a flat-bottomed, non-metallic bowl if you don't have a rice tub.

Spread the rice over the flat bottom of the tub with a spatula. Slowly add the vinegar mixture by pouring it onto the spatula and allowing it to flow onto the rice. Quickly mix the rice and vinegar together with the spatula, using a slicing action to coat the grains of rice evenly and to separate them.

Fan the shari rice mixture to cool the surface temperature to about skin temperature. Transfer the cooled shari rice into a container and cover with a damp cloth. Keeping the temperature of the shari rice slightly warm is crucial; when cooled, the starch in the rice looses its absorbency and the texture in the mouth will be uneven and hard. Too hot, on the other hand, will impair the freshness of the topping on the rice, so keeping shari rice at around body temperature is ideal.

Serves 4

miso soup

see variations page 48

Miso is the very soul of Japan. Made with traditional methods, it is rich in vitamins and high in protein and also has an amazing ability to rid the body of toxins. If you're feeling a little run down in the morning, miso soup is a great pick-me-up!

1 block of silken tofu
1 oz. wakame seaweed
1 qt. dashi stock (page 44)

2 oz. of mugi miso paste (per bowl)
2 chopped scallions

Strain the tofu and cut the tofu block into 1/3-in. cubes. Rehydrate the wakame seaweed in a bowl with cold water for about 5 minutes or until soft. (Read the packet, as sometimes the wakame doesn't need rehydrating.) Squeeze the water out and chop into 3/4-in. lengths.

Place the dashi in a saucepan and bring to a boil. Stir a little of the dashi water into the miso paste to thin it before adding it to the dashi water. Lower the heat and stir as the soup simmers gently. Place the tofu cubes and wakame in miso bowls, ladle out the miso soup, and garnish with chopped scallion.

Serves 2

gari pickled ginger

see variations page 49

Historically, when much of the available arable land was given up to rice production, pickles were used as a means of staying healthy and were pretty much the only vegetable consumed throughout the winter months when fresh vegetables became scarce. Another reason for their popularity is their infinite versatility. They are made with many different types of vegetables; regional variations are great sources of local pride. Pickles have come to signify the end of a meal in Japan. Their appearance is so anticipated that even after a full meal the Japanese will feel that something is missing until the tsukemono arrive. Pickled ginger, however, holds a slightly different place in the world of pickles. Gari, pickled sushi ginger, as it is known exclusively in sushi restaurants, is made to be eaten sparingly between the different sushi rather than at the end of a sushi meal.

7 oz. fresh, young ginger, peeled and sliced into
   long, thin diagonals
4 tsp. sea salt

3/4 cup rice vinegar
4 tsp. sugar
3/4 oz. red shiso leaf

Place the slices of ginger in a bowl, sprinkle on the salt and leave for about an hour. Transfer the ginger slices into a sterilized jar. In a separate container, stir together the rice vinegar and sugar until the sugar has dissolved.

Pour the rice vinegar liquid over the ginger pieces in the jar. Add the red shiso leaves, put the lid on the jar, and store in the refrigerator at least overnight, and up to a week. It is the addition of the red shiso leaf that gives gari its pale pink color.

Serves 4

yuzu mayonnaise

see variations page 50

The use of mayonnaise in sushi started in California and was later introduced into Japan. I'm not a big fan of smothering my sushi in any form of mayonnaise, mostly because it, in my opinion, serves only to mask the subtle flavors of the ingredients and detracts from the texture. I would thus recommend using the following recipes as dipping sauces (alternatives to soy sauce) rather than adding it to maki rolls, but your own palate will let you know how you feel about using it.

2 yolks from large eggs
1 tsp. mustard powder
1 clove of crushed garlic
9 fl. oz. peanut oil

1 tsp. rice vinegar
1 tsp. light soy sauce
1/2 tsp. yuzu zest

Make sure all the ingredients are at room temperature. Place the egg yolks in a bowl and add the mustard powder and garlic. Mix well together. With an electric beater in one hand (or a wire whisk) and a jug of peanut oil in the other hand, start to add the oil to the egg yolk mixture drop by drop. At the beginning, be sure that each drop of oil is whisked in before adding the next drop to prevent curdling.

After a while the mixture will start to thicken. When about half the oil is mixed in, add the rice vinegar. Once all the oil is thoroughly whisked in, add the soy sauce and yuzu zest and mix well. Set aside and chill.

Makes about 1 1/4 cups

teriyaki sauce

see variations page 51

Beware of just how much sugar or sweetener you are using in your Japanese dishes and where possible use an alternative such as honey or apple juice, or buy good brands of mirin (outside of Japan I have only come across the Clearspring brand, which is truly heavenly).

roasted chicken thigh bones
roasted leek tops
10 fl. oz. dark soy sauce

1/2 cup sake
1/2 cup hon-mirin
2 tbsp. honey

You can either grill or roast the chicken bones and leeks. Add the roasted chicken bones and leek tops to a saucepan then combine all the liquid ingredients except the honey in the pan. Bring it to a boil and gently simmer for 20 minutes until the sauce has thickened. Add the honey and stir for a further 5 minutes.

It is worth noting that most Japanese recipes I have looked at recommend equal portions of mirin to soy and one-third volume of sugar, so if the above recipe isn't what you are looking for, feel free to play around with the ratios or add sugar!

Makes about 2 1/2 cups

ponzu

see variations page 52

Ponzu is a tangy citrus-flavored soy sauce, and its simple clean flavor complements most whitefish, as well as "shiny" ones such as horse mackerel. It can also be used in more modern dishes and is great in salad dressings.

1 1/2-in. square piece of konbu kelp
8 tbsp. soy sauce

8 tbsp. rice vinegar
2 tbsp. lemon juice

Combine all the ingredients and leave overnight in a refrigerator. Remove the konbu before using the ponzu.

Makes about 1 cup

saikyo miso

see variations page 53

This incredibly simple topping is best known for doing amazing things to eggplant!

1/2 cup sake
1/2 cup mirin

7 oz. white miso paste
3 tbsp. sugar

Bring the sake and mirin to a boil in a saucepan over high heat and boil for a few seconds to cook off the alcohol.

Turn down the heat and add the miso paste, mixing with a wooden spoon. When the miso has dissolved, turn up the heat again and add the sugar, stirring constantly to prevent the sauce from sticking. Remove from heat once the sugar has dissolved.

Makes about 3 cups

ceviche sauce

see variations page 54

The following recipes are inspired by the flavors of South America. Ceviche cooking has been championed in Japanese restaurants by Nobuyuki Matsuhisa at his restaurant, Nobu. The ceviche sauce is best paired with chopped, leftover pieces of shellfish or whitefish. The citrus and oil semi-poach the raw flesh. It is good Zen not to waste, and this recipe helps achieve that.

1 red onion	2 tbsp. dashi
3 cloves garlic	1 tbsp. soy sauce
1 fresh jalapeño	2 tsp. lime juice
1 red chile with seeds	3 tbsp. olive oil
1 shiso leaf	5 fl. oz. shiso juice
1 scallion stem	sprinkle of sesame seeds

Roughly chop the onion, garlic, jalapeño, chile, shiso leaf, and scallion. Mix the dashi, soy, lime juice, olive oil, and shiso juice. Blend all the sauce ingredients together.

Sprinkle in the sesame seeds.

Makes about 1 1/2 cups

dashi stock

see variations page 55

Dashi is the basic stock in Japan. Unlike its Western counterparts, dashi is quick and easy to make, relying, as so much of Japan's food does, on the integrity, quality, and skill that has gone into producing its ingredients.

1 oz. or 1 piece of dried kelp konbu about   1 1/2 qt. water
   4-in. long   1 tbsp. katsuo dried bonito flakes

Do not wipe the white glutamate deposits from the surface of the konbu — this is precisely the umami flavor that you seeking to extract. Place the konbu in a saucepan with the water and bring to a boil.

Simmer for 15–20 minutes until the liquid is reduced. Remove the konbu and bring to a boil again. Add 4 tablespoons of cold water and the katsuo flakes. Let infuse for 5 minutes. Strain the liquid to remove the katsuo and set aside the clear dashi.

Makes about 1 1/2 quarts

variations

tsuma — sashimi decoration

see base recipe page 27

shiso leaf
Shiso leaf is a quintessentially Japanese sushi ingredient. Its beautiful light green or red leaves impart color and vibrancy to a plate of sashimi, and it has a fragrance and flavor quite unlike any other herb. Shiso has powerful antibacterial properties, which is always a consideration when dealing with raw ingredients that can easily deteriorate. It contains a lot of vitamins and minerals that are a good boost to the immune system, are particularly good in treating allergies, and have a beneficial effect on the skin.

mixed seaweed tsuma
There are virtually no calories in seaweed, and it contains high amounts of vitamins A, B, C, and E in addition to minerals and, in particular, iodine, as well as calcium, magnesium, and iron. Moreover, it is high in omega-3. Combining different colored seaweeds makes a really attractive tsuma or even a salad.

hijiki seaweed & daikon tsuma
Hijiki is brown seaweed and looks like stems of tea on a plate. Its lustrous black contrasts well with the gleaming white of the radish. It usually comes in dried form and, depending on the brand, generally needs simmering for about 30 minutes before using in the tsuma.

cucumber & daikon tsuma
Peel a length of cucumber the same way as the daikon radish and mix together.

variations

shari sushi rice

see base recipe page 28

genmai brown rice
Replace the uncooked rice with genmai short-grain brown rice. The water will be less milky in the washing process. Follow the same cooking and mixing steps but double the amount of water used in the rice cooking process.

gomoku rice or 5-grain rice
Gomoku rice translates as "five grain," or "five things," but in fact you can choose any number of different grains to suit your taste. Grains to chose from might include millet, adzuki bean, black rice, soybean, red rice, black sesame, and white sesame. Follow the same cooking steps but double the amount of water.

low-sugar shari rice
Generally, the ratio of vinegar to rice is about 15 percent, but you can adjust the salt and sugar as you like. You'll find the right balance as you become more practiced, but salt amounts typically range from a small pinch to about 3/4 teaspoon per 7 tablespoons of uncooked rice, and sugar from 3/4 tablespoon to as much as 4 teaspoons.

sake & konbu shari rice
If you are eager to retain a good flavor but also reduce the amount of sugar or salt, then add a 3-in. strip of konbu dried kelp to the rice pot before cooking, or add a little sake rice wine to the mixture. Both are very traditional practices in Japan.

variations

miso soup

see base recipe page 30

red miso, burdock & carrot
Prepare the basic recipe, replacing mugi miso with red miso paste. Blanch a few julienned pieces of burdock and carrot, and add a splash of sesame oil.

red miso, shiitake mushroom & nira garlic shoots
Prepare the basic recipe, replacing mugi miso with red miso paste. Add a few blanched pieces of shiitake mushroom and nira garlic shoots.

saikyo miso & snapper
Prepare the basic recipe, replacing mugi miso with saikyo miso. Pour a little boiling water over 1-in. lengths of a whitefish fillet. Chop a few trefoil mitsuba leaves or chives and add them and a few spinach leaves.

saikyo miso & lotus root
Prepare the basic recipe, replacing mugi miso with saikyo miso. Cut a lotus root into 1/2-in. thick slices, chop these into quarters, and lightly blanche them. Add two pieces of lotus root to each bowl of miso soup.

gochujang miso stew
Prepare the basic recipe. Stir in a teaspoon of gochujang Korean chili paste. For each bowl of miso, add a few blanched, 3/4-in. square chunks of Chinese cabbage, a small bunch of enoki mushrooms, a couple of 3/4-in. lengths of nira garlic chives, and 4 pieces of diced tofu.

gari pickled ginger

see base recipe page 32

salted cucumber pickles
Prepare the basic recipe, replacing ginger with small Japanese cucumbers. Slice the cucumbers, and cover with salt. Leave under a heavy weight at least overnight.

vinegared & wasabi cucumber pickles
Prepare the basic recipe, replacing ginger with cubed cucumber. Smear with a little wasabi.

daikon white radish in sake pickles
Prepare the basic recipe, replacing ginger with sliced white radish and replacing half the rice vinegar with sake rice wine.

eggplant pickles
Prepare the basic recipe, replacing ginger with small Japanese eggplants.

kanpyo calabash gourd pickles
Prepare the basic recipe, replacing ginger with calabash. The pieces of calabash often come in dried form, so they first need to be rehydrated overnight in water. Replace rice vinegar with sake rice wine and salt. Add a few sesame seeds.

chinese cabbage & chile pickles
Prepare the basic recipe, replacing ginger with slices of salted Chinese cabbage and chopped chile.

variations

yuzu mayonnaise

see base recipe page 34

wasabi mayonnaise
Prepare the basic recipe, replacing yuzu zest with freshly grated wasabi root. Omit the mustard powder.

gochujang Korean chili mayonnaise
Prepare the basic recipe, omitting the mustard powder and replacing yuzu zest with up to 1 tablespoon of gochujang (Korean chili paste).

smoked paprika mayonnaise
Prepare the basic recipe, omitting the mustard powder and rice vinegar, and replacing yuzu zest with 1/4 teaspoon smoked paprika, juice of 1 lemon, and freshly ground black pepper.

sweet chili mayonnaise
Prepare the basic recipe, omitting the mustard powder. Replace yuzu zest with up to 1 tablespoon of Thai sweet chili sauce.

tonkatsu mayonnaise
Prepare the basic recipe, omitting the mustard powder and replacing yuzu zest with up to 1 tablespoon of tonkatsu sauce, or Worcestershire sauce.

teriyaki sauce

see base recipe page 36

teriyaki with gochujang (korean chili) sauce
Prepare the basic recipe, adding 3 tablespoons of gochujang with the honey.

thickened teriyaki sauce
Prepare the basic recipe, adding a teaspoon of kuzu starch to the sauce when simmering.

chile & sesame teriyaki sauce
Prepare the basic recipe, adding two teaspoons of sesame oil and 1 finely chopped red chile.

ginger teriyaki sauce
Prepare the basic recipe, adding a teaspoon of oroshi grated ginger.

variations

ponzu

see base recipe page 39

wafu salad dressing
Prepare the basic recipe, adding 6 tablespoons peanut oil, 1 tablespoon mirin, 1 tablespoon toasted sesame oil, and a little Japanese mustard.

tamari wafu dressing
Prepare the basic recipe, replacing the soy sauce with tamari for a wheat-free ponzu and add to the above recipe.

ponzu butter
Heat a tablespoon of butter in a pan. Once melted, add 2 tablespoons of ponzu and combine together over a low heat. This is a nice sauce to spoon over some of the sushi recipes that use meat or cooked shellfish.

tofu sesame salad dressing
Combine half a block of tofu with 1 tablespoon of toasted sesame oil, 2 tablespoons of sunflower oil, 3 tablespoons of ponzu, a little white miso paste, and minced garlic.

yuzu vinaigrette
Combine 2 teaspoons Dijon mustard, 1/3 cup sesame oil, 1/2 cup olive oil, 1/2 cup rice vinegar, 1 cup light soy sauce, 1 cup yuzu juice (or 1/2 cup lime juice if you can't find yuzu juice), 1/2 cup dashi, 4 tablespoons sugar or 4 tablespoons concentrated apple juice, and 1/2 medium onion finely chopped.

variations

saikyo miso

see base recipe page 40

sesame dressing

Thoroughly mix together 1 tbsp. goma tare tahini paste, 1/2 tbsp. sesame oil, 1 tbsp. soy sauce, 1/4 tsp. grated garlic, 1/4 tsp. grated ginger, 3/4 tbsp. rice vinegar, 1/2 tbsp. runny honey, a squeeze of lemon juice, and up to 2 tbsp. dashi stock. Add dashi stock to adjust the viscosity of the sauce.

creamy spicy white miso dip

Combine equal portions of saikyo miso with wasabi mayonnaise.

variations

ceviche sauce

see base recipe page 43

jalapeño salsa
Combine 2 finely chopped jalapeños, 7 tablespoons finely chopped onions, 1 oz. chopped cilantro, 1 oz. chopped flat-leaf parsley, 1 tablespoon soy sauce, 1/2 tablespoon rice vinegar, 1/4 teaspoon chili oil, and 1 tablespoon olive oil. Serve immediately.

korean chili sauce
Combine 3 tablespoons chili pepper paste (gochujang), 3 tablespoons vinegar, 1/2 tablespoon sugar, 1 tablespoon apple juice, 1 tablespoon sesame seeds, 1 tablespoon chopped scallion, and 1/2 bowl sesame oil.

apple-mustard sauce
Grate half an apple, a 1 1/2-in. length of ginger, and half a small onion (all oroshi style). Combine 1/2 cup of rice vinegar, 2 1/2 tablespoons grapeseed oil, 2 1/2 tablespoons toasted sesame oil, 2 tablespoons sake, and 4 teaspoons soy. Mix this liquid together with the oroshi ingredients, and then add a teaspoon of shichimi pepper, a teaspoon of toasted sesame seeds, and a heaping tablespoon of coarse-grain mustard.

variations

dashi stock

see base recipe page 44

vegetarian dashi stock
Soak two pieces of 6-in. long konbu and three dried shiitake mushrooms in about
1 1/2 quarts of water for at least half an hour. Then bring the liquid to a boil and simmer
gently for 15 minutes. Strain off the konbu and shiitake and set aside the vegetarian dashi
to cool.

tempura dipping sauce
In a saucepan, combine 1 cup dashi stock, 1/4 cup hon-mirin, and 1/4 cup soy sauce and mix
well. Bring to a boil on medium heat for 2 minutes.

nigiri sushi

The nigiri form of sushi is the classic style formed in
Edo (old Tokyo) in the 1820s with the advent of the
wider use of rice vinegar and sugar. It is hailed as
being the first example of the type of sushi that is
familiar to us today and in Japan is by far the most
commonly found in a typical sushi dinner.

salmon nigiri

see variations page 79

Ironically, when I first visited Japan in the 1980s, it wasn't possible to obtain salmon, a freshwater fish, in its raw form. This changed with the huge increase of farmed salmon in the 1990s, and salmon is now one of Japan's top five fish for eating. If you are going to use wild salmon, it is advisable to choose a whole salmon of about 9 pounds, and one before it has laid eggs, after which the flesh deteriorates significantly.

1 lb. fillet of salmon, skin on
1 1/2 lbs. shari rice (page 28)

soy sauce, to serve
wasabi, to serve

Remove the skin from the fillet. Hold the knife at a 45 degree angle to the fish and cut diagonal slices so that each piece has a slight taper. Applying a quite firm pressure with your fingers to the fillet, slice through the remainder of the fillet to form even slices.

Use the technique described on pages 20–21 to shape the shari rice ball and make your salmon nigiri. The finished salmon nigiri shape should be even and, if you've managed to handle the shari and salmon as little as possible, the nigiri should look as though it were about to swim away!

Typically, one would serve two nigiri sushi at a time. With a bowl of soy sauce in place, gently dip the sushi, salmon side down, into the soy sauce and eat immediately.

Makes about 45 pieces

marinated tuna nigiri

see variations page 80

Before the introduction of flash-freezing at sea, the Japanese often used the following technique as a means of preserving fish. As tuna stocks dwindle, the quality of tuna becomes increasingly irregular, but this marinade will greatly improve any tuna recipe.

1 cup soy sauce
1/2 cup mirin
1/2 cup sake
1 lb. tuna fillet
bowl of ice water

1 1/2 lbs. shari rice
chopped scallion
grated ginger
wasabi, to serve
soy sauce, to serve

Place the soy sauce, mirin, and sake in a saucepan and gently bring to a boil. Remove from heat and let cool. Cut the fillet of tuna into 3-in. long blocks. Place the blocks in a colander and cover with a clean cloth. Pour boiling water over the cloth-covered fish. When the surface of the fish has changed color, turn it over and repeat on the other side. Remove the cloth and immediately place the tuna in a bowl of ice water. Pat dry when cooled. Place the tuna blocks in the soy marinade and allow to soak in the refrigerator for 30–40 minutes. Using a slender-bladed yanagiba knife, hold the knife parallel to the fish, and cut slices from the block. Each slice should be around 2 1/2–3 in. long, 1 in. wide, and 1/4 in. thick, and weigh about 1/2 oz. each.

Cut the fish at right angles to its sinews. Otherwise, whole slices of nigiri topping may be white in appearance and hard and chewy. Make each nigiri in the same way as described on pages 20–21. Top each nigiri with a sprinkling of chopped scallion and grated ginger. Serve with wasabi and soy sauce.

Makes about 20 pieces

mackerel, scallion & ginger nigiri

see variations page 81

Mackerel's richness in omega-3 oils makes it tasty and good for us. A vinegar marinade accentuates its natural flavors, and also eradicates the bacteria often found in oily fish.

2 mackerel fillets of about 6–7 oz. each (from
    large mackerel of preferably over 2 lbs.)
4 tbsp. of sea salt
1 cup of rice vinegar

1 3/4 cup shari rice
chopped scallion
grated ginger

Fillet the mackerel in the sanmai 3 part method (page 16). Place the mackerel fillet skin-side down in a bamboo colander covered with half of the salt. Sprinkle the remainder of the salt evenly on top of the mackerel fillets and place in the refrigerator for 45 minutes until the salt is dissolved. Then rinse the fish in cold water and pat dry. Place the fillets skin-side down in a clean flat-bottomed container and pour the rice vinegar over to cover the fillets entirely. Set aside to marinate for between 30 minutes and 1 hour, depending on the size of the fish. (The flesh should be faintly red inside; if totally white, it has been left too long). Remove the fillets from the vinegar and drain. Place on a chopping board and gently run your fingers across the flesh to find the bones. Remove the bones with a tweezer.

Cover with plastic wrap or a damp cloth and store in the refrigerator until you are ready to make your nigiri. Slice the mackerel into about 1/8-in. thick pieces, weighing about 1/2 oz. each. Make diagonal slashes in the skin to reveal the contrast between the shiny silver skin and the redder flesh inside. Make the mackerel nigiri with the technique shown on pages 20–21. Top with chopped scallion and grated ginger.

Makes about 20 pieces

lobster tail & yuzu mayonnaise nigiri

see variations page 82

Crustaceans look wonderful on top of nigiri sushi, adding color and texture to a sushi feast. They are one of the few ingredients in nigiri that are often cooked.

1/2 lb. lobster, boiled (just the tail is fine)
1 3/4 cups shari rice (page 28)
nori sheet

4 oz. yuzu mayonnaise (page 34)
chopped scallion

Have a large saucepan ready with enough water to cover the lobster and a bowl of ice water at hand. Live lobsters can be humanely killed beforehand by putting them in a plastic bag in the freezer for about two hours.

Scald the lobster in boiling water for 4 minutes, then plunge into the ice water. Remove the meat from the shell when cooled. Cut the tail into pieces about 3 in. long each, and 1 in. wide. Make each nigiri in the same way as described on pages 20–21.

Run a band of nori around the nigiri to secure the lobster chunk if it doesn't feel as though it will stay in place (not shown in our photo). Top each nigiri lobster morsel with a teaspoon of yuzu mayonnaise and chopped scallion.

Makes about 20 pieces

tea-smoked salmon nigiri

see variations page 83

Smoked fish aren't traditionally used in sushi, but if you have any doubts about the quality or freshness of your fish, then smoking it is a tasty and safe way to prepare it. Raw salmon, mackerel, and some other fish present a significant risk of the parasite anisakis: only freezing these for at least 24 hours at temperatures beyond most home freezers' capability (below -24°F) will ensure safety. It's best to leave this to professionals.

3 tbsp. hojicha green tea leaves
3 tbsp. uncooked rice
5 tsp. brown sugar
5 tsp. sesame seeds
1 clove garlic, unpeeled

1/2 lb. salmon fillet
1 3/4 cups shari rice (page 28)
4 oz. wasabi mayonnaise (page 50)
shiso cress or mustard and cress

Mix the hojicha, rice, sugar, sesame seeds, and garlic together for the smoking mixture. Cover the base of a wok with aluminum foil and empty the smoking mixture onto it. Place the colander or steamer into a wok. Place the salmon into the steamer, cover, and smoke for 8 minutes over a medium heat. If you don't have a steamer or colander, cover the mix with aluminum foil and lay the salmon on top.

Don't peek until the 8 minutes have gone by. It's best to take the wok outside before you lift the lid as there will be a lot of smoke. Take off the lid, and when the smoke has gone, you will be left with wonderful hot tea-smoked salmon. When cool enough to cut, slice into pieces, each about 3 in. long, 1 in. wide, and 1/4 in. thick. Make each nigiri in the same way as described on pages 20–21. Top each nigiri with a teaspoon of wasabi mayonnaise and shiso cress or mustard and cress.

Makes about 20 pieces

foie gras & pomegranate nigiri

see variations page 84

Most unconventional, but decadent and delicious. Take your time to find foie gras reared without cruelty — I'm sure a happy goose will taste better, and you'll feel better. You can always try this with Japan's famed "foie gras of the sea," monkfish liver (page 206).

1/2 lb. foie gras (goose liver)
potato flour, for coating
1/2 cup rice vinegar
1 cup soy sauce
1/2 cup mirin

truffle oil
1 tbsp. pomegranate seeds
1 3/4 cups shari rice (page 28)
nori strips
chopped leek

Heat a sharp knife under boiling water and cut the foie gras into 3/4-in. nigiri slices. Coat with potato flour. Preheat a non-stick skillet over medium heat without using oil. Sear the foie gras on each side until golden brown with a crispy surface. It might be prudent to do it piece by piece, taking care not to break them. Drain on paper towels.

In the same skillet, leave a little of the foie gras oil and add the rice vinegar, soy, and mirin. Over high heat, boil the sauce gently to reduce. Add a splash of truffle oil. When the sauce has reduced and thickened, add some pomegranate seeds.

Make the nigiri rice balls as described on pages 20–21 and put them on a chopping board. Carefully arrange the foie gras on top and secure with a strip of nori (not shown in our photo). Top with chopped leek and a few more pomegranate seeds. Spoon the sauce over the nigiri when ready to eat.

Makes about 20 pieces

yubiki scalded red snapper nigiri

see variations page 85

Snappers and breams are generally referred to as tai in Japan, and cover as many as 200 different species. The common thread between them from a sushi perspective is their firm and even-textured flesh, with a relatively low fat content and simple yet distinctive flavor. They are held in great regard in Japan. Simple, salt-broiled tai is common at New Year and birthday celebrations.

1/2 lb. red snapper fillet
sea salt, for preparation and garnish
bowl of ice water

1 3/4 cups shari rice (page 28)
zest of one lime

Snapper has a delicious fatty skin, but its toughness makes it difficult to eat. For this reason, a technique known as yubiki, where the skin is scalded, is commonly used. Only the skin is cooked, while the flesh underneath remains raw.

Place the fillet of snapper on a bamboo colander with the skin facing upward and sprinkle with sea salt. Place a thin cloth over the fish and pour boiling water over it, working from the tail to the head (in the opposite direction of the line of the scales). Quickly immerse in a bowl of ice water.

When cool enough to cut, slice into pieces about 3 in. long, 1 in. wide, and 1/8 in. thick. Make each nigiri the same way described on pages 20–21. Top with a sprinkle of lime zest and sea salt.

Makes about 20 pieces

aburi hamachi yellowtail

see variations page 86

Aburi, or seared sushi, was developed nearly a century ago in Japan. The act of applying fire directly and lightly, as a sear, is known to enhance the natural flavors of the fish.

1/2 lb. hamachi yellowtail fillet	grated Parmesan cheese
1 3/4 cups shari rice (page 28)	chopped chives

Requires a blowtorch. Slice the yellowtail fillet into pieces about 3 in. long, 1 in. wide, and about 1/8 in. thick. Make each nigiri the same way as described on pages 20–21.

Place the nigiri on a stainless steel tray and sprinkle them with the grated Parmesan cheese. Gently blowtorch the surface of the yellowtail until it becomes charcoaled on the outside. Top with chopped chives.

Makes about 20 pieces

broiled shishito pepper nigiri

see variations page 87

Vegetarian sushi is quite limited in traditional Japanese sushi bars but has become increasingly popular in the West with the desire to rely less heavily on animal protein and go for low-calorie options. Certainly, a sushi lunch is low in calories, in spite of all the sugar and rice! A typical sushi lunch box meal contains fewer than 500 calories.

20 shishito peppers, or Spanish pedron peppers
1 cup dashi (page 44)
1 tbsp. light soy sauce
3/4 tbsp. mirin

1 tbsp. sake
1 3/4 cup shari rice (page 28)
4 oz. smoked paprika mayonnaise (page 50)

This recipe starts with one of the classic forms of Japanese cooking, a nimono or simmered/poached dish. Trim the stems of the peppers. In a saucepan, add the dashi stock, soy sauce, mirin, and sake, and bring to a gentle boil. Add the peppers and simmer gently for about 2 minutes. This is your basic nimono dish. Remove the peppers from the saucepan and place under a broiler for 1 minute, or until the skins of the peppers are lightly browned.

Make each nigiri in the same way as described in on pages 20–21. Top with a dot of smoked paprika mayonnaise.

Makes about 20 pieces

octopus nigiri

see variations page 88

Octopus and squid are often eaten raw in Japan, but can also be cooked to tenderize the flesh, which we will explore in this recipe.

3 lbs. whole octopus
1 tbsp. sea salt
1 cup dark soy sauce

1/2 cup mirin
1/2 cup sake
1 3/4 lb. shari rice (page 28)

Choose a large whole octopus (the smaller species are not suitable for sushi). A large frozen octopus will work well, too. Cut where the tentacles join the head and remove the beak with your fingers. Turn the head inside out and remove the innards. Rinse well under cold water and remove any fibrous tissue. There are a number of ways to tenderize the octopus, none of which seem very conventional! Either pound the octopus flesh with half a raw daikon or, when boiling, add a tea bag. Fill a large saucepan with enough water to cover the octopus, add a tablespoon of sea salt, and bring to a boil. Tentacles first, place the octopus in the boiling water. Bring to a boil again, then lower the heat and simmer gently with the lid on for about 30 minutes. To keep the skin undamaged, make sure that the octopus isn't jiggling about. Take the saucepan off the heat and leave the octopus in the water to cool.

Bring the soy, mirin, and sake gently to a boil. Lower the heat and simmer to reduce the liquid for about 15 minutes. Remove from heat and let cool. Cut the octopus tentacles into nigiri-shaped slices and make the nigiri as described on pages 20–21. Wrap a piece of nori around the octopus. With a pastry brush, lightly brush the octopus with the soy mixture.

Makes about 40 pieces

scorched plaice nigiri

see variations page 89

Yuzu is a citrus fruit unique to Japan, with no foreign equivalent. The flesh is rarely used, but the zest and juice is valued as much for its aroma as for its flavor.

1/4 medium white daikon (radish)
1 tsp. yuzukosho

1/2 lb. plaice (flatfish) fillet
1 3/4 cups shari rice (page 28)

Using a flat grater, grate the white radish until it becomes almost a paste. Add a heaping teaspoon of yuzukosho and mix together. You can use any flatfish in this dish; choose one that is local and sustainably caught in your area. Even though the fish is scorched, a fresher fish will not only taste better but its flesh will retain a better texture. Fillet as you would for a nigiri. Fillet the plaice using the gomoi oroshi technique described on page 18. Slice into nigiri neta (pieces) of about 1/2 oz. each. Score the top of each neta with a sharp knife to make even lines across the top. This adds to both the appearance and texture of the sushi. Make the nigiri as described on pages 20–21.

When you have your nigiri ready, place two skewers under the broiler or on top of a barbecue grill until scorching hot. Carefully pick up the hot skewers and with them scorch the top of each nigiri to produce charcoaled lines running across the flesh. Top with the grated radish mixture.

Makes about 20 pieces

tataki beef & caviar nigiri

see variations page 90

"Tataki" means to pound, and refers to the finely minced ingredients, often ginger or garlic, that are served with meat or fish for added flavor. These ingredients are usually served alongside, or used to marinate, seared meat or fish.

1 tbsp. oroshi ginger	vegetable oil, for frying
1 tbsp. oroshi garlic	1 3/4 cups shari rice (page 28)
1 leek	skewers, for broiling
14 oz. beef fillet, around 1 1/2-in. thick	1/2 oz. caviar

Using a flat grater, grate the ginger then garlic until they become almost a paste. Finely slice a 2-in. length of leek. Trim the beef fillet. Heat a little vegetable oil in a small pan and quickly pan fry each side of the fillet for around 1 minute on each side, so as to brown the outside but leave the inside pink.

Slice the fillet into 3-in. long, 1 1/2-in. wide, very thin slices. Make the nigiri as described on pages 20–21. Once you have your nigiri, take two skewers and leave under the broiler or on top of a BBQ until scorching hot. Carefully pick up the scorching hot skewers and scorch the top of each nigiri to produce charcoaled lines running across the flesh. Top each nigiri with a half a teaspoon of caviar, small dabs of oroshi grated ginger and garlic, and finely chopped leek.

Makes about 20 pieces

tamago omelet nigiri

see variations page 91

You tend to hear that the Japanese have no sweets, but they do. The place for sweets is with a cup of tea between meals. Thus, it is not uncommon to end a sushi dinner with a piece of sweet tamago sushi.

1 tsp. sugar
2 fl. oz. dashi (page 44)
2 tsp. soy sauce
1 tsp. mirin
6 eggs

vegetable oil, for frying
1 3/4 cups shari rice (page 28)
nori sheet
wasabi, to serve

Prepare the omelet as described on page 189. Make the nigiri as described on pages 20–21. Cut a 1/2-in. wide, 3-in. long strip of nori and make a band around the center of the tamago. This is a traditional way of securing a topping that is difficult to hold in place, and is not a sign of an amateur!

If you would like this dish to be vegetarian, make your dashi using konbu kelp and shiitake mushroom, and not katsuo boshi bonito flakes as described on page 44.

Makes about 10 pieces

salmon nigiri

see base recipe page 57

tuna nigiri
Replace the salmon with yellowfin tuna.

sea bass, scallion & ginger nigiri
Replace the salmon with sea bass. Generally, choosing a large adult sea bass will provide a more creamy texture. Using a flat grater, grate a 1/8-in. piece of ginger; finely chop half the scallion using, ideally, the part that moves from white to green. Place a small sprinkle of each at the center top of the sea bass.

turbot, ume plum & chives nigiri
Replace the salmon with turbot. With a small teaspoon carefully put a small dab of ume plum paste on the center top of the turbot and top with finely chopped chives.

hamachi yellowtail & chives nigiri
Replace the salmon with hamachi, an increasingly popular, usually farmed fish in the West. The creamy texture of this fish means that little needs to be done to it. Simply top with chopped chives.

horse mackerel, scallion & ginger nigiri
Replace the salmon with horse mackerel and top with scallion and ginger, as in the second variation above.

variations

marinated tuna nigiri

see base recipe page 58

lemon sole in soy sauce, mirin & sake nigiri
Replace the tuna with a fillet of lemon sole. Once skinned, slice into thin, 1/8-in. thick strips and reduce the marinating time to 20–30 minutes.

gray mullet in soy sauce, mirin & sake nigiri
Replace the tuna with a fillet of gray mullet. Slice into thin, 1/8-in. thick strips. Reduce the marinating time to 20–30 minutes.

tiger shrimp & shari vinegar nigiri
Replace the tuna with a boiled tiger (jumbo) shrimp. Marinate it, in the refrigerator, in the shari vinegar mixture used to make sushi rice (page 28).

tiger shrimp in gari ginger juice nigiri
Replace the tuna with a boiled tiger (jumbo) shrimp. Omit the boiling water stage. Pickled gari ginger from a Japanese store comes vacuum packed in its own juices, or you can make your own pickled ginger (page 32). These vinegary ginger juices are good to marinate the shrimp in for about 30 minutes in the refrigerator.

variations

mackerel, scallion & ginger nigiri

see base recipe page 61

herring in rice vinegar nigiri

Replace the mackerel with herring and marinade for about 30 minutes only.

sardines in rice vinegar nigiri

Replace the mackerel with sardines and marinade for about 45 minutes.

aji horse mackerel in rice vinegar nigiri

Replace the mackerel with horse mackerel (*Trachurus japonicus*), a much underrated fish outside of Japan. Marinade for about 30 minutes only.

anchovy in rice vinegar nigiri

Replace the mackerel with anchovy and shorten the marinating time to about 10 minutes. If you are using canned anchovies take care to rinse them of their salt, and remove the backbone and tail.

variations

lobster tail & yuzu mayonnaise nigiri

see base recipe page 62

tiger shrimp nigiri
Replace the lobster with tiger (jumbo) shrimp, prepared in the way described on page 225.

ama ebi sweet shrimp nigiri
Replace the lobster with ama ebi sweet shrimp. There are two commonly used shrimps for ama ebi: the Alaskan pink shrimp (Pandaluseous makarov) or botan shrimp (Pandalus nipponensis), found more frequently off the West coast of the United States. Remove the head and shell gently so as not to break the tail, aiming to take as much of the intestinal tract with it. Remove thoroughly any remainder of the intestinal tract. Soak in a bowl of salted water for 5 minutes then rinse. Amaebi has a distinctive enough flavor of its own, but it is nice to add a dab of mayonnaise. Wasabi mayonnaise suits this shrimp better than yuzu.

scallop & shiso nigiri
Staying with the raw style of the variation above, prepare scallops in the way described on page 100. Cut a shiso leaf in half and lay it on top of the shari rice ball before topping it with the raw scallop. Again, scallops are wonderfully sweet in their own right, but a dab of wasabi mayonnaise adds another tasty dimension.

akagai red clam nigiri
Replace the lobster with akagai red clam. The part of the clam eaten here is the exterior mantle that houses the clam's body. Try to find a Japanese grocer to prepare it for you. Best eaten without mayonnaise.

variations

tea-smoked salmon & cress nigiri

see base recipe page 64

hamachi yellowtail, jalapeño & cilantro salsa garnish nigiri
Replace the salmon fillet with yellowtail, and replace the wasabi mayonnaise and chives with cilantro–chile salsa.

tea-smoked salmon, soy, mirin, kimchee & shichimi 7-spice chili pepper garnish nigiri
Combine equal portions of light soy sauce and mirin, and add a teaspoon of kimchee base. Using a pastry brush, coat the tea-smoked salmon top with the mixture, and finish with a sprinkle of shichimi.

smoked salmon, cream cheese & chives nigiri
Replace the tea-smoked salmon with thinner slices of smoked salmon. Top each nigiri of smoked salmon with a dab of cream cheese that has been beaten to make it smooth, and chopped chives.

avocado, jalapeño & cilantro salsa nigiri
A delicious vegetarian alternative is to replace the tea-smoked salmon with a slice of avocado. This goes really well with the jalapeño salsa.

variations

foie gras & pomegranate nigiri

see base recipe page 66

seared duck & chives nigiri

Prepare the duck breast in the same way as the foie gras, using a little oil to fry it. There is no need to coat the duck breast in flour. Decorate with chopped chives for more color.

seared beef & pink peppercorn nigiri

Prepare the beef fillet the same way as the foie gras, using a little oil to fry. There is no need to coat the beef in flour. Add pink peppercorns instead of pomegranate to the sauce.

seared hamachi yellowtail & wasabi nigiri

Prepare the yellowtail fillet the same way as the foie gras, using a little oil to fry. There is no need to coat the fish in flour. Add a hint of wasabi powder instead of pomegranate to the sauce.

seared tuna, korean gochujang chili sauce & scallion nigiri

Prepare the tuna fillet in the same way as the foie gras, using a little oil to fry. There is no need to coat the fish in flour. Add a teaspoon of Korean chili sauce instead of pomegranate to the sauce, and top with chopped scallion.

ankimo monkfish liver nigiri

Prepare the ankimo, "foie gras of the sea," as described on page 206, coating it in potato flour. Add sansho pepper to the sauce, and top with chives.

variations

yubiki scalded red snapper nigiri

see base recipe page 69

turbot, oroshi daikon white radish & yubiki nigiri
Replace the red snapper fillet with turbot and substitute the lime and sea salt garnish with grated white radish.

lemon sole, sea salt & lime yubiki nigiri
Replace the red snapper with lemon sole.

red mullet, sea salt & lemon yubiki nigiri
Replace the red snapper with red mullet. The red mullet is a beautiful example of the yubiki technique because the red scales contrast so strikingly with the white flesh. Mix the sea salt with lemon zest for the garnish.

flounder, scallion & ginger yubiki nigiri
Replace the red snapper with flounder and top with grated oroshi ginger and finely chopped scallion.

variations

aburi hamachi yellowtail

see base recipe page 70

tataki tuna & gochujang korean chili mayonnaise aburi nigiri
Replace yellowtail with tuna, blowtorch, and top with a dot of gochujang chili mayonnaise (page 50).

sole, yuzukosho & oroshi daikon aburi nigiri
Replace yellowtail with sole (or another firm, white, flatfish). Top with yuzukosho paste.

salmon, saikyo miso & chives aburi nigiri
Replace yellowtail with salmon, blowtorch, top with saikyo miso (page 40), and blowtorch again. Garnish with chopped chives.

sea urchin uni roe & sea salt aburi nigiri
Replace yellowtail with sea urchin. Blowtorch, add a tiny sprinkle of good sea salt, and secure this with a band of nori.

tofu & saikyo miso sauce aburi nigiri
Replace yellowtail with chunks of tofu cut into nigiri shapes, blowtorch, and top with saikyo miso (page 40). Blowtorch again to create a classic tofu dengaku dish.

variations

broiled shishito pepper nigiri

see base recipe page 73

nimono shiitake mushroom & smoked paprika mayonnaise nigiri
Replace peppers with shiitake mushrooms. If using dried shiitake, simmer one large mushroom for each nigiri, cooking them for a little longer than you would fresh ones.

nimono enoki mushrooms & smoked paprika mayonnaise nigiri
Replace peppers with enoki mushrooms. Simmer a small bunch of enoki for each nigiri, being careful not to break their bases.

avocado & smoked paprika mayonnaise nigiri
Replace broiled peppers with slices of avocado; a large, sliced avocado should make five nigiri.

marinated tofu nigiri, ginger & scallion
Replace peppers with firm tofu in soy marinade (page 58). Lightly broil 1 marinated tofu block, cut into 1/2-in. slices, and top with pickled ginger (page 32).

shiso & ume plum nigiri
Take one whole shiso leaf, make a nigiri sushi form, and top with a dab of tangy ume paste.

inari tofu nigiri
Replace peppers with inari tofu. Wash and cut a slice of inari tofu and top with scallion and ginger.

variations

octopus nigiri

see base recipe page 74

octopus & nori nigiri
Plain and simple: omit the soy brushing at the end.

octopus, chile, oroshi daikon & lime nigiri
Omit the soy, mince the daikon radish with finely chopped red chile and lime zest for your daikon oroshi topping.

squid, ume plum & scallion nigiri
Replace octopus with squid as prepared on page 17. Broil the squid until the surface turns opaque. Cut the squid into nigiri shapes and top with ume plum paste and chopped scallion.

squid, chili & lime nigiri
Replace octopus with squid as prepared on page 17. Broil the squid until the surface turns opaque. Cut the squid into nigiri shapes and top with finely chopped chile and lime zest.

squid & shiso nigiri
Replace octopus with squid as prepared on page 17. Broil the squid until the surface turns opaque. Cut the squid into nigiri shapes, brush with the soy marinade, and garnish with chopped shiso leaf.

variations

scorched plaice nigiri

see base recipe page 76

scorched sea bass, daikon oroshi & yuzukosho nigiri

Replace the plaice with sea bass fillet.

scorched salmon & shichimi 7-spice pepper nigiri

Replace the plaice with salmon fillet, scorching for a little longer as it has a fattier, denser flesh. Sprinkle with shichimi pepper.

scorched tuna, sea salt & black pepper nigiri

Replace the plaice with tuna fillet. After scorching, simply top with crushed black pepper and sea salt.

scorched king crab & wasabi mayonnaise nigiri

Replace the plaice with meat from 1 king crab. Boil the crab and cut the shell with scissors to extract the legs in one piece. As each crab piece will form one whole nigiri, take care not to break the flesh when removing it. Secure with a strip of nori. Once scorched, top with wasabi mayonnaise (page 50).

scorched scallop & shiso nigiri

Replace the plaice with scallops as prepared on page 110. Top with torn shiso leaf.

variations

tataki beef & caviar nigiri

see base recipe page 77

tataki quail & spring onion nigiri
Prepare the basic recipe, replacing beef with a quail breast. Sear and top with finely sliced
spring onion and the oroshi grated ginger and garlic.

tataki duck & pomegranate nigiri
Prepare the basic recipe, replacing beef with a duck breast. Sear and top with oroshi daikon
grated white radish, mixed with a few pomegranate seeds and a splash of soy sauce.

chorizo & smoked paprika mayonnaise nigiri
Prepare the basic recipe, replacing beef with 1 medium link chorizo sausage, pan fried and
cut into long diagonal pieces, and top the nigiri with a dab of smoked paprika mayonnaise
and oroshi grated garlic.

variations

tamago omelet nigiri

see base recipe page 78

tamago with adzuki bean sweet nigiri
Prepare the basic recipe, adding a tablespoon of cooked, sweetened adzuki beans to the
uncooked egg mixture.

yokan adzuki bean jelly sweet nigiri
Yokan is a thick red bean paste, and makes an unconventional and sweet topping for
sushi. You can buy koshian, adzuki bean paste, from Japanese grocery stores. Slice the yokan
into pieces 2 in. long, 1 1/2 in. wide, and 1/2 in. thick, and place on top of the nigiri rice.
Secure with a band of nori.

yokan aduki bean jelly & chestnut sweet nigiri
Prepare the recipe above, adding a few finely chopped boiled sweet chestnuts and
1/2 teaspoon honey to top the nigiri.

gunkan battleship sushi

Some ingredients are softer and more liquid than most, and these need help staying atop the rice. Hence, they are held in place by a strip of nori. The appearance of this strip resembles old battleships, and hence the name. When making gunkan, remember that moist hands are good when touching the shari rice, but it is best to have dry hands when handling the nori.

ikura salmon roe classic gunkan

see variations page 112

There are a few gunkan toppings that are seen far more often than others, and ikura is probably the most common. Bears hunting salmon in the rivers of Canada can often be seen savoring their prey's nutritious, delicious roe. Once you've tasted it for yourself, you'll know that the bears are on to something.

4 tsp. salmon roe	4 tsp. shari rice (page 28)
3 tbsp. soy sauce	1 nori sheet
3 tbsp. sake	wasabi

Place the salmon roe in a small bowl and cover with the soy and sake. Marinate in a refrigerator for at least 4 hours. Pour off the soy and sake, taking care not to break the eggs.

To create the gunkan shape, first cut the nori into 6-in. long and 1-in. wide strips (one sheet of nori will cut into 6 strips). Moisten your hands with vinegared water. Take a ball of rice the size of a golf ball and shape it into an oblong with rounded edges. Dry your right hand and place a nori strip in it. With the rough side facing the rice, press the end of the nori to the rice and wrap it all around the rice ball. Take one grain of rice and crush it and use this to paste down the overlapping ends of the nori. Dab a little wasabi on top of the rice, and add 1 teaspoon of the salmon roe, taking care not to moisten the sides of the nori.

Serve immediately, otherwise the nori becomes soggy and difficult to eat. Because of this, if you are making a selection of sushi, it is best to leave gunkan until the last. Salmon roe is already quite salty, but if you'd like to add soy sauce, pour it on top of the roe directly from a dispenser, rather than dipping the gunkan. Gunkan are usually served in pairs.
Makes 1 gunkan

aji no tataki horse mackerel gunkan

see variations page 113

Often there are smaller bits of fish fillets left over that are difficult to use in nigiri or sashimi but make perfect gunkan ingredients. They are chopped into small pieces and spooned on top of the gunkan.

1 tbsp. horse mackerel fillet
1 tsp. scallion
1 tsp. minced grated ginger
1 tsp. ponzu sauce (page 39)

4 tsp. shari rice (page 28)
nori sheet
wasabi

Prepare the horse mackerel fillet in the sanmai 3-piece method as described on page 16. It is only a small fish, but you can use the fatter parts of the fillet for nigiri sushi. Chop the smaller ends into small pieces.

The word tataki means to strike or pound, so here we have beaten, or minced, horse mackerel. Thinly slice the scallion and mix with the horse mackerel and minced ginger along with the ponzu sauce. Make the gunkan as described on page 93, and spoon over the horse mackerel mixture. You won't need soy sauce.

Makes 1 gunkan

crab & avocado gunkan

see variations page 114

I have seen Japanese and French friends sit for hours over a plate of freshly boiled crabs, picking happily away at the flesh — slow food to be lingered over and appreciated. If you're not happy with waiting, it is easy to buy processed crabmeat, and this is fine to use in gunkan.

1 tbsp. crabmeat
4 tsp. shari rice (page 28)
nori sheet

1 tbsp. avocado
soy sauce, to serve

Any edible crab can be used in gunkan, though many tend to use spider crab for its sweeter flesh (there are a number of varieties of spider crab around the world, so ask your fishmonger for one with the sweetest flesh). Steam the crabs whole over high heat for about 20 minutes (less for smaller crabs). Separate the crab body from the shell and remove the meat. Mix the brown and white crabmeat together, adjusting the ratio according to your preference.

Make the gunkan shape as described on page 93. Chop the peeled avocado into small pieces. Gently combine the chopped avocado with the crabmeat, or use decoratively fanned slices of avocado, and spoon the crabmeat onto the gunkan.

Pour the soy sauce on top of the crab directly from a dispenser rather than dipping the gunkan in a bowl of soy sauce.

Makes 1 gunkan

shrimp tempura gunkan

see variations page 115

A variety of textures is an important consideration in Japanese food, and making tempura toppings for a gunkan is a tasty, though unconventional option.

1 tiger shrimp
4 tsp. shari rice (page 28)
nori sheet
wasabi
chili mayonnaise (page 50)
2 tsp. chopped chives

for the batter (to coat up to 30 shrimp)
1 cup all-purpose flour plus a little extra
    for coating
1 large egg
1 1/2 cups ice water and ice cubes
vegetable oil for deep-frying

Prepare the shrimp as described on page 225. Now make the tempura batter. The secret is to not beat the batter too vigorously, so mix the flour, egg, and ice water with chopsticks and leave lumps of flour unblended. You can also add ice cubes if you like.

Heat the vegetable oil in a small deep pan to 335°F. If you don't have a thermometer, you can test the temperature by flicking in a drop of batter. It should sink and then rise; if it just sinks it is too cool, and if it rises right away it is too hot. Coat the shrimp in a little flour. Remove the excess flour, then dip it into the batter. Carefully drop it into the hot oil for about 3 minutes or until the batter has turned golden. Remove the shrimp with chopsticks or a draining spoon and leave to drain on a wire rack or a paper towel.

Make the gunkan shape as described on page 93. Chop the shrimp tempura into 3/4-in. long pieces. Spread a layer of chili mayonnaise over the rice, and top with pieces of the shrimp. Decorate with chopped chives.
Makes 1 gunkan

octopus ceviche &
red pepper gunkan

see variations page 116

South American chefs put ceviche sauces on the map, and though not at all
traditional in Japan, the slightly poached effect is delicious. Like the tataki preparation,
this sauce can be used on the thinner ends of a fish that are left over when making
nigiri or sashimi.

4 tsp. shari rice (page 28)
nori sheet
wasabi
1 tbsp. octopus

1 tsp. chopped red pepper
2 tsp. ceviche sauce (page 43)
shiso cress or mustard and cress

Make the gunkan shape as described on page 93.

Prepare the octopus as described on page 74. Dice the octopus and combine with the
chopped red pepper and the ceviche sauce.

Spoon the octopus mixture over the rice and decorate with shiso cress or mustard and cress.

Makes 1 gunkan

panfried duck, pomegranate, soy sauce & honey gunkan

see variations page 117

The pomegranate, soy, and honey sauce is somewhere in between hoisin sauce and sour cherry.

1 duck breast
salt and pepper
7 oz. yuzu mayonnaise (page 34)
3 tbsp. soy sauce
1 tbsp. honey

1 tbsp. pomegranate seeds, reserving some
    for decoration
7 tbsp. chopped chives
1 3/4 cup shari rice (page 28)
4 nori sheets

Clean and trim the duck breast. Heat a small non-stick skillet and, without using oil, panfry the breast skin-side down, turning it and cooking until it is golden brown on both sides. Remove from the heat, wrap in aluminum foil, and leave for 10 minutes. Remove the foil, slice into thin slices, and season with salt and pepper. Bake in an oven on a high heat of 400°F for just a minute.

Combine the yuzu mayonnaise with the soy sauce, honey, pomegranate seeds, and chopped chives. Make the gunkan shape as described on page 93. Spoon the yuzu mayonnaise on top of the rice. Arrange a slice of the duck breast on top and decorate with a few pomegranate seeds.

Makes 20 gunkan

uni sea urchin & burnt creamy miso mayonnaise gunkan

see variations page 118

Miso dengaku, a creamy sauce made with white miso, is perhaps best known served on eggplant. It is always a popular dish. Miso is strongly flavored so in this recipe it is combined with a wasabi mayonnaise. You can mix and match as you like.

1 sea urchin
1 thin slice of cucumber
1/2 tsp. wasabi mayonnaise (page 50)
1/2 tsp. saikyo miso (page 40)

4 tsp. shari rice (page 28)
1 nori sheet
shredded nori

Place the sea urchin on a thin slice of cucumber. This is to steady it while it is under the broiler. Put it on a broiler pan and spoon 1/2 teaspoon of wasabi mayonnaise on the left side of the sea urchin and 1/2 teaspoon of saikyo miso on the right. Broil until the surface turns golden brown.

Make the gunkan shape as described on page 93. Carefully lift the cucumber and urchin and place on top of the rice. Garnish with shredded nori.

Note: You can achieve the same effect using a blowtorch lightly over the topping of the mayonnaise and miso.

Makes 1 gunkan

squid with ginger, sake, soy sauce & sesame gunkan

see variations page 119

Light pan-frying is a quick and easy cooking method — particularly for shellfish and white fish — as there's no need to marinate first.

1/2 lb. squid tentacles
1 tbsp. vegetable oil
2 tsp. toasted sesame oil
2 tbsp. dashi (page 44)
2 tbsp. soy sauce
2 tbsp. sake

1 tbsp. mirin
4 tsp. grated ginger
1 3/4 cup shari rice (page 28)
sesame seeds
wasabi, for serving

Prepare the squid as described on page 17. You can use the body as well if you like but on a gunkan the tentacles look particularly tempting with their bright color and curly shapes. Cut the tentacles into 3/4-in. cubes.

Heat the oil in a skillet and add the prepared squid. Combine the sesame oil, dashi, soy sauce, sake, mirin, and ginger, and heat gently in a small saucepan. Pour it over the squid and simmer for 2–3 minutes. Drain the squid and, once cool, mix with the sesame oil. Bring the remaining liquid to a high heat to reduce.

Make the gunkan shape as described on page 93. Put the squid on top of the rice, add a light sprinkle of sesame seeds, and drizzle a little of the reduced soy mixture over the squid. There is no need to dip this gunkan in soy before eating.

Makes 20 gunkan

shiitake mushroom gunkan

see variations page 120

Shiitake mushrooms are renowned for their intense flavor and aroma and are becoming increasingly popular in the West for their good taste and health benefits. They are thought to help fight cancer and have long been used in Chinese medicine to boost the immune system. Moreover, they have nearly zero calories and plenty of vitamin D. In spite of being a classic Japanese ingredient, it is not often found in sushi.

1–2 shiitake mushrooms (dried ones are fine)
6 tbsp. dashi (page 44)
1 tbsp. mirin

1 tbsp. soy sauce
4 tsp. shari rice (page 28)
chopped chives

Rehydrate your mushrooms in a bowl of water for 30 minutes if you are using dried ones. Clean and cut off any hard part of the stem if using fresh ones.

In a small pan, combine the dashi, mirin, and soy sauce, and bring to a gentle boil. Simmer the shiitake for 3 minutes or until soft and bouncy to the touch. Drain and cool. Chop into slices or chunks, as you prefer.

Make the gunkan shape as described on page 93. Arrange the mushrooms on top of the rice and add a light sprinkle of chives.

There is no need to dip this gunkan in soy before eating.

Makes 1 gunkan

scallop with shiso gunkan

see variations page 121

This is a classic combination, where the subtle balance of green in the shiso and white of the scallop appeal to the eye, and the sweet creaminess of the scallop contrasts with the fragrant sharpness of the shiso leaf.

1 scallop
4 tsp. shari rice (page 28)
chopped shiso leaf

It is preferable to use live scallops in their shell for this as they are eaten raw, though you can substitute with frozen scallop meat. Extract the scallop from the shell. Remove the beard and innards and discard. Rinse the scallop in cold water and drain.

Make the gunkan shape as described on page 93. Chop the scallop into small cubes and mix lightly with the chopped shiso leaf.

This gunkan is best eaten with a little soy sauce.

Makes 1 gunkan

variations

ikura salmon roe classic gunkan

see base recipe page 93

mentaiko pollock roe gunkan
Replace salmon roe with pollock roe, which is much smaller and is marinated in sake, soy, and chili to produce a red, smoky chili mixture.

masago capelin roe gunkan
Replace salmon roe with capelin roe. The roe are small, and the membrane quite tough, so they give a popping sensation when chewed.

kazunoko herring roe gunkan
Replace salmon roe with herring roe. It is quite firm, with an amazingly crunchy texture.

uni sea urchin gunkan
Replace salmon roe with fresh uni. Only the gonads of the urchin are eaten in sushi. It has an extraordinary rich creaminess with an ocean-fresh scent.

caviar gunkan
Replace salmon roe with caviar. Opt for sustainably raised caviar and mix with a little wasabi.

variations

aji no tataki horse mackerel gunkan

see base recipe page 94

salmon tataki & avocado gunkan
Replace mackerel with finely chopped ends of salmon fillet mixed with one slice of avocado chopped into similar-size pieces. Top the gunkan with the mixture and serve with wasabi mayonnaise (page 50).

tuna tataki, scallion & wasabi mayonnaise gunkan
Replace mackerel with finely minced yellowfin tuna. Mix with 1 teaspoonful of thinly sliced scallion and wasabi mayonnaise to top the gunkan.

plaice tataki, ume plum & chive gunkan
Replace mackerel with finely chopped ends of plaice fillet. Mix with a little ume plum paste and chopped chives to top the gunkan.

hamachi yellowtail tataki & shiso gunkan
Replace mackerel with finely chopped ends of yellowtail fillet. Mix with a little chopped shiso leaf and ponzu sauce (page 39) to top the gunkan.

ama ebi sweet shrimp tataki & avocado gunkan
Prepare the sweet shrimp as described on page 225, and cut into small pieces. Chop one slice of avocado into similar-size pieces and add a little wasabi mayonnaise. Spread the mixture over the shrimp.

variations

crab & avocado gunkan

see base recipe page 97

lobster & chive gunkan
Replace crabmeat with lobster as prepared on page 62. Chop into 3/4-in. square pieces and mix with chopped chives to top the gunkan.

shrimp & yuzu zest gunkan
Replace crabmeat with shrimp as prepared on page 225, and combine with the zest of yuzu (or lemon) to top the gunkan.

crabmeat & scallion gunkan
Prepare the basic recipe, omitting the avocado and adding 2 teaspoons of finely chopped scallion to the crab meat.

raw lobster, oroshi daikon & ponzu gunkan
Replace crabmeat with finely chopped raw lobster meat. Combine with a teaspoon of ponzu sauce (page 39) and grated daikon radish to top the gunkan.

langoustine & avocado gunkan
Replace crabmeat with boiled langoustine chopped into 1/3-in. square pieces. Combine with the avocado and a teaspoon of yuzu mayonnaise (page 34) to top the gunkan.

variations

shrimp tempura gunkan

see base recipe page 98

monkfish tempura, lime & sansho pepper gunkan
Replace shrimp with monkfish tail. Sprinkle sansho pepper and sea salt in the flour before frying. Sprinkle over lime zest to serve.

squid tempura & chile gunkan
Replace shrimp with 1/2 oz. of small pieces of squid. Top with finely chopped red chile.

lobster tempura & lemon gunkan
Replace shrimp with lobster tail cut into 3/4-in. pieces and mixed with lemon zest.

scallop tempura & shiso gunkan
Omit shrimp. Deep-fry a scallop. You can use the coral as well as the white meat if you like. Chop into small pieces and sprinkle with torn shiso leaf to top the gunkan.

crab claw tempura, chives & yuzu mayonnaise gunkan
Replace shrimp with the meat of a crab claw. Place on top of the gunkan. Top with chives and yuzu mayonnaise.

oyster tempura & chile gunkan
Omit shrimp. Tempura one whole oyster. Place it on top of the gunkan and garnish with chopped chile.

variations

octopus ceviche & red pepper gunkan

see base recipe page 100

plaice ceviche & scallion gunkan
Replace octopus with chopped raw plaice and combine with chopped chives and a spoonful of ceviche sauce to top the gunkan.

salmon, jalapeño salsa & avocado gunkan
Replace octopus with chopped raw salmon and replace red pepper with chopped avocado and a spoonful of jalapeño salsa (page 54). Combine to top gunkan.

hamachi yellowtail with jalapeño salsa & pink peppercorn gunkan
Replace octopus with chopped raw yellowtail and combine with a spoonful of jalapeño salsa (page 54), a few pink peppercorns, mustard & cress, or shiso cress.

turbot ceviche with cilantro & chive gunkan
Replace octopus with chopped raw yellowtail and combine with a spoonful of ceviche sauce and chopped cilantro and chives.

cuttlefish ceviche & cucumber gunkan
Replace octopus with chopped raw cuttlefish and combine with a spoonful of ceviche sauce and a few slices of thinly sliced cucumber.

variations

panfried duck, pomegranate, soy sauce & honey gunkan

see base recipe page 102

panfried tuna, chives & korean chili sauce gunkan

Prepare the basic recipe, replacing duck with a fillet of tuna, using a little oil to fry. Make the gunkan using Korean chili sauce (page 54), and garnish with chopped chives.

baked scallop & ponzu butter gunkan

Omit the frying stage and replace duck with 10 large scallops. Season the scallops with salt and pepper and bake at 400°F for 3 minutes. Combine 4 tablespoons yuzu mayonnaise (page 34) with 2 tablespoons ponzu (page 39) and top the gunkan with shredded nori.

panfried beef with teriyaki & yuzukosho oroshi gunkan

Prepare the basic recipe, replacing duck with a tender cut of beef such as loin or rib, using a little oil to fry. Omit soy sauce, honey, and pomegranate. Brush the beef with teriyaki sauce (page 36), and decorate with a dab of yuzukosho paste mixed with grated daikon white radish.

baked foie gras gunkan

Omit the frying stage and replace duck with foie gras, coated in potato flour. Season with salt and pepper and bake at 400°F for 3 minutes. Omit soy sauce, pomegranate, and honey and decorate with chopped mitsuba leaf (Japanese wild parsley).

uni sea urchin & burnt creamy miso mayonnaise gunkan

see base recipe page 105

oyster & dengaku white miso gunkan
Replace urchin with a raw oyster. Spoon over a little saikyo miso sauce (page 40) and either broil or blowtorch until browned.

mentaiko pollock roe & creamy wasabi sauce gunkan
Replace urchin with 1 tablespoon pollock roe. Spoon over a little wasabi mayonnaise and either broil or blowtorch. Top with shredded nori.

shirako cod milt & scallion gunkan
Replace urchin with 1/2 oz. shirako cod milt on a slice of cucumber. Sprinkle with chopped scallion and spoon on a little smoked paprika mayonnaise (page 50). Then either broil or blowtorch.

octopus & dengaku white miso gunkan
Replace urchin with 1/2 oz. boiled octopus. Spoon over a little saikyo miso sauce (page 40) and either broil or blowtorch until browned.

duck with dengaku white miso gunkan
Replace urchin with a 1/2 oz. slice of duck breast, prepared as on page 102. Spoon over a little saikyo miso sauce, and either broil or blowtorch until browned.

squid, with ginger, sake, soy sauce & sesame gunkan

see base recipe page 106

razor clam with yuzu, sake, sesame & soy sauce gunkan
Prepare the basic recipe, replacing squid with 7–10 razor clams cut into
3/4-in. length pieces. Replace the ginger with yuzu juice or zest.

shrimp with chile, sake, sesame & soy sauce gunkan
Prepare the basic recipe, replacing squid with 10 large raw tiger shrimp cut into
roughly three pieces each. Replace the ginger with chopped chile.

lemon sole with ginger, sake, sesame & soy sauce gunkan
Prepare the basic recipe, replacing squid with a 10 1/2 oz. fillet of lemon sole,
chopped into larger pieces than basic recipe and coated with potato flour before
frying to help keep its shape.

monkfish with cilantro, sake, sesame & soy sauce gunkan
Prepare the basic recipe, replacing squid with monkfish. Replace the ginger with
chopped cilantro.

chicken with ginger, sake, sesame & soy sauce gunkan
Prepare the basic recipe, replacing squid with chicken cut into 1-in. cubes,
simmering for 4–5 minutes.

shiitake mushroom gunkan

see base recipe page 109

enoki mushroom gunkan
Replace the shiitake mushrooms with enoki mushrooms and sprinkle with sesame seeds.

bamboo shoot gunkan
Replace the shiitake mushrooms with bamboo shoot. Simmer the bamboo shoot in the dashi–soy sauce mixture and sprinkle with sesame seeds.

asparagus, green bean & green pepper gunkan
Replace the shiitake mushrooms with asparagus, green beans, and green pepper; they will need less simmering time than the shiitake.

lotus root & shiitake mushroom gunkan
Prepare the basic recipe. Add lotus root chunks to the pan; add the shiitake 2 minutes later.

okra gunkan
Remove the tops and stems of the okra and replace the shiitake mushrooms with topped okra. Reduce the simmering time to 1–2 minutes. Allow 1–2 okra for each gunkan.

samphire with butter teriyaki gunkan
Replace the shiitake mushrooms with cleaned samphire. Reduce the simmering time to 1–2 minutes, and add a small knob of butter to the sauce towards the end.

scallop with shiso gunkan

see base recipe page 110

cuttlefish & shiso gunkan
Replace scallop with cuttlefish. Chop into small cubes and mix with the shiso leaf to top
the gunkan.

turbot & shiso gunkan
Replace scallop with 1/2 oz. turbot fillet chopped into small cubes. Mix with the shiso to top
the gunkan.

yellowtail & shiso gunkan
Replace scallop with 1/2 oz. yellowtail fillet chopped into small cubes. Mix with the shiso to
top the gunkan.

scallop, ceviche & shiso gunkan
Prepare the base recipe, adding a spoonful of ceviche sauce (page 43). Garnish with
torn shiso.

hosomaki

Hosomaki, meaning "thin roll" in Japanese, are simple and easy to make. The hallmark of a good maki maker is to have the filling right in the center of the roll. These simple canapés look attractive at any dinner party. If you are preparing the hosomaki some time before you plan on eating them, be careful that you don't roll the maki too tightly; sushi rice swells with time, and as the nori is absorbent, a tightly made roll will squeeze the rice and the maki will become hard.

ume plum & cucumber hosomaki

see variations page 136

Ume plum is a quintessential Japanese fruit used as an ingredient. The Japanese plum is close to the Western apricot. The plums are pickled in salt, and later in shiso leaf, to produce an exceptionally tart pickle. They contain a lot of citric acid, which is deemed to aid digestion. Often served on a bowl of rice at breakfast, they hold a special place in Japan's culinary heart.

1/2 nori sheet
1/4 cup shari rice (page 28)
wasabi

1 tsp. ume plum paste
1 tbsp. julienned cucumber

Place your bamboo rolling mat with the knotted side facing up. Place the non-shiny side of the nori facing up on your mat, with the longest edge nearest you. Dampen your hands, take the rice, and shape it into a narrow log on top of the nori. Being careful to not apply too much pressure so that the grains of rice remain undamaged, evenly spread the rice outward, leaving a gap of about 1/4 in. at the top — the side farthest away from you. Dab some wasabi in a line over the center of the rice and spread it slightly.

With a teaspoon spread the ume plum paste over the center of the rice and place the julienned cucumber on top of the plum. Holding on to either side of the nori, at the side nearest you, roll the mat away from you with your index fingers and thumbs. Roll tightly until the near end of the nori reaches the far edge, leaving bare the strip of rice-free nori. Cover the roll with the mat (but not the rice-free gap), press gently to shape; you can make them square or round as you like. Trim the edges; cut in half, then into 6 pieces.

Makes 1 roll, or 6 pieces

oshinko pickled daikon hosomaki

see variations page 137

Pickles and vegetables often comprise the ingredients in a hosomaki. Pickles are an essential part of a Japanese meal, and they are typically served with a bowl of rice and miso soup, signifying the end of a good dinner. Each region has its own variations of pickling, but as a rule, while pickles in the West are made with vinegar, which softens them, Japanese pickles tend to be crunchy as they are usually made with salt.

1/2 nori sheet	6-in. length Oshinko pickle
1/4 cup shari rice (page 28)	wasabi

Oshinko pickles are very traditional and are commonly found in hosomaki. You may recognize them by their bright yellow centers. You can buy oshinko but be careful to purchase a good brand, as they are often full of a whole host of additives, flavorings, and colorings.

Roll the maki as described on page 123, making sure to center the strip of oshinko.

Makes 1 roll, or 6 pieces

asparagus & bacon teriyaki hosomaki

see variations page 138

Using just a little rice and meat is a modern interpretation of the traditional hosomaki.

1 stem asparagus
1/2 nori sheet
3 tbsp. shari rice (page 28)
Japanese mustard

1 slice of thinly sliced unsmoked bacon
oil for frying
1 tsp. teriyaki sauce (page 36)

Blanch the asparagus. Roll the maki as described on page 123, replacing the wasabi with Japanese mustard. Put the asparagus in the center. Wrap the filled nori with the bacon slices and secure with toothpicks or skewers.

Heat the oil and lightly panfry the maki on all sides. Remove the toothpicks and cut into 6 pieces. Serve with teriyaki sauce.

Makes 1 roll, or 6 pieces

brown rice & bamboo hosomaki

see variations page 139

It is not at all common to use brown rice in sushi, but here, as with onigiri, brown rice works really well. There is less starch in brown rice, so it tends to be less sticky than white rice. (See variations for uses of other grains.) In the basic recipe you can add all kinds of different vegetables to the rice, chopping them finely.

4 fl. oz. soy sauce
2 fl. oz. sake
4 fl. oz. dashi
2 fl. oz. apple juice or 2 oz. sugar
4-in. piece bamboo
2 shishito, or Spanish pedron peppers

1 medium carrot
4 water chestnuts (canned is fine)
1 3/4 cups genmai rice (page 47)
2 nori sheets
wasabi

Combine the soy sauce, sake, dashi, and apple juice in a small saucepan. Add the bamboo, shishito, carrot, and water chestnuts and bring to a boil, then simmer for about 2 minutes until the liquid has nearly evaporated.

Drain the vegetables and cool. When they have cooled, chop them into small cubes and mix with the brown rice.

Roll the maki as described on page 123, but as there is no filling in this roll, take care not to press down too heavily.

Makes 6 rolls, or 36 pieces

goat cheese, chive & walnut hosomaki

see variations page 140

Dairy is not traditionally eaten in Japan, but deep-fried Brie wrapped in nori has popped up on plenty of menus in Japan's izakaya bars recently. The combination of umami rich cheeses, such as Parmesan and Roquefort, with nori, also rich in umami, make powerful savory flavors.

1 tsp. walnuts
1/2 nori sheet
1/4 cup shari rice (page 28)
wasabi

1 tbsp. calpressi goat cheese (or any soft goat cheese)
1 tsp. chives

Toast the walnuts in a pan, remove from heat, and chop. Roll the maki as described on page 123, spreading the goat cheese along the center. Sprinkle the toasted walnuts and whole lengths of chive over the cheese.

Makes 1 roll, or 6 pieces

fried shrimp hosomaki

see variations page 141

Try to make the maki when you are ready to eat them; they are so much nicer when the fillings are still warm.

2 ebi tiger/jumbo shrimp
1 in. vegetable oil for deep frying
1 tbsp. potato flour

1/2 nori sheet
1/4 cup shari rice (page 28)
wasabi

Prepare the shrimp as described on page 225, but don't marinate.

Heat 1 in. of good vegetable oil in a small saucepan to 355°F.

Dust the shrimp with potato flour and deep fry for 3 to 4 minutes. Roll the maki as described on page 123, making sure to center the shrimp.

Makes 1 roll, or 6 pieces

tekkamaki — tuna hosomaki

see variations page 142

While the origins of tekkamaki, the tuna sushi roll, is disputed, the commonly accepted theory is that it was designed for Go, a Japanese chess-like game, so that the players could eat without getting their hands sticky or disrupting the game.

1/2 nori sheet
1/4 cup shari rice (page 28)

wasabi
6-in. length raw tuna

Roll the maki as described on page 123, making sure to center the strip of tuna. If you like wasabi, now is the time to be generous with it!

Makes 1 roll, or 6 pieces

yellowtail tempura hosomaki

see variations page 143

If you are keen on sushi for its fresh, cleansing flavors and low calorie content, then this one isn't for you! But deep-frying a whole roll provides a great contrast between hot and cold, crispy and soft — both contrasts that the Japanese celebrate in their food.

1/2 nori sheet
1/2 cup shari rice (page 28)
wasabi
6-in. length yellowtail fillet
vegetable oil, for deep-frying
shiso cress
2 tsp. tempura sauce (page 55)
1 tsp. grated oroshi ginger

1 tsp. grated oroshi daikon white radish

batter
9 oz. all-purpose flour, plus a little extra
    for coating
1 large egg
1 3/4 cups iced water and ice cubes

Make the hosomaki with the yellowtail in the center as described on page 123. When you have finished rolling it, compress each end, and dip each end into the flour. Now make the tempura batter. The secret is not to beat the batter too vigorously, so mix the flour, egg, and iced water with a chopstick and leave lumps of flour unblended. You can also add ice cubes if you like. Heat the vegetable oil in a small deep pan to 340°F. Very lightly flour the outside of the hosomaki by rolling it on a floured plate. Dip the whole roll into the batter, then toss into the hot oil for around 3 minutes, or until the batter has turned golden. Remove the maki with a stainless mesh spoon and leave to drain on a wire rack or kitchen paper. Cut the maki into 6 pieces. Decorate with shiso cress. Pour the tempura sauce into a small dipping bowl, and place along side it a small plate with the grated radish and ginger, added just before dipping the hosomaki roll.

Makes 1 roll, or 6 pieces

variations

ume plum & cucumber hosomaki

see base recipe page 123

ume plum & shiso hosomaki
Prepare the basic receipe. Cut a shiso leaf in half and arrange on top.

natto fermented soybean & scallion hosomaki
Omit the ume plum paste. Roll the maki with a heaping teaspoon of natto. Sprinkle with chopped scallion.

natto fermented soybean & okra hosomaki
Omit the ume plum paste. Roll the maki with a heaping teaspoon of natto. Sprinkle with finely chopped okra.

ume plum & daikon white radish hosomaki
Prepare the basic recipe, replacing cucmber with a 6-in. long strip of daikon. Roll with a teaspoon of ume plum paste.

bamboo hosomaki
Prepare the basic recipe, replacing cucmber with a strip of boiled bamboo as prepared on page 247. Sprinkle with sesame seeds.

oshinko pickled daikon hosomaki

see base recipe page 125

kappamaki hosomaki
Replace oshinko with raw cucumber. Sprinkle with sesame seeds.

kanpyo pickled calabash gourd hosomaki
Replace oshinko with pickled calabash in the center. Prepare the pickle as described on page 32, replacing ginger with calabash.

enoki mushroom hosomaki
Replace oshinko with enoki mushrooms, blanched and marinated in soy sauce and rice vinegar for 30 minutes. Top with sesame seeds.

avocado & sesame hosomaki
Replace oshinko with slices of avocado with a sprinkle of sesame seeds.

asparagus hosomaki
Replace oshinko with one blanched stem of asparagus and roll with a smear of wasabi mayonnaise (page 50).

okra & sesame hosomaki
Replace oshinko with blanched okra, marinated in soy sauce and rice vinegar for 30 minutes, and roll with a sprinkle of sesame seeds.

variations

asparagus & bacon teriyaki hosomaki

see base recipe page 126

foie gras & asparagus hosomaki
Panfry the foie gras as described on page 66. Season with a dash each of yuzu juice and truffle oil and wrap, with the asparagus and foie gras on the inside. There is no need to fry the whole maki.

pancetta (italian bacon) & fig hosomaki
Replace asparagus with 1 whole fig, cut into quarters. Wrap the roll in pancetta slices. There is no need to fry this maki.

pancetta (italian bacon), mozzarella & chive hosomaki
Replace asparagus with pencil-size pieces of mozzarella and roll the maki sprinkled with chopped chives. Wrap the roll in pancetta slices. There is no need to fry this maki.

marinated beef hosomaki
Prepare the basic recipe, omitting asapargus. Sear a 1/2 oz. slice of marbled tender beef (such as sirloin or rib-eye) in a pan as described on page 251, and plunge into ice water. Marinate in soy sauce and mirin for at least an hour, then cut into pencil-size lengths and place on the inside of the roll with plenty of wasabi.

variations

brown rice & bamboo hosomaki

see base recipe page 128

brown rice, red rice, ume plum, shiso & edamame

Prepare the basic recipe, replacing half the genmai rice with red rice and cooking both together. Omit bamboo, vegetables, and chestnuts. Mix rice mixture with 3 1/2 oz. boiled, chopped edamame beans. Spread a little ume plum paste across the center of the mixed rice, add a few torn shiso leaves, and roll.

brown rice, sesame, adzuki, red rice & millet

In Japan and Japanese grocery stores, you can actually buy this mix ready to steam. If you can't find it, replace 1/3 genmai rice with red rice and 1/3 with millet, and steam together. Omit bamboo, vegetables, and chestnuts. Add 2 tablespoons canned adzuki beans, and sprinkle with black and white sesame seeds, and roll.

brown rice, ham, peas & carrot

Replace bamboo, vegetables, and chestnuts with 3 oz. chopped ham, 1 medium carrot, chopped and blanched, and 2 oz. boiled peas. Mix vegetables with brown rice, sprinkle with sesame seeds, and roll.

brown rice with kinpira burdock & carrot

Omit bamboo, vegetables, and chestnuts. Cook the kinpira and carrot as described on page 252. Mix 1 3/4 oz. finely chopped onion, rice mixture, kinpira mixture, and roll.

variations

goat cheese, chive & walnut hosomaki

see base recipe page 130

gruyère & sunblush tomato hosomkai
Replace goat cheese with a pencil-size stick of Gruyère. Roll with some halves of sunblush (semi-sun-dried) tomatoes. This is a classic umami-rich combination.

mozzarella & sunblush tomato hosomaki
Replace goat cheese with a pencil-size stick of mozzarella and roll with some halves of sunblush tomato.

roquefort & endive hosomaki
Replace goat cheese with a pencil-size stick of Roquefort and roll with a couple of leaves of endive.

gorgonzola & celery hosomaki
Replace goat cheese with a pencil-size stick of gorgonzola and roll with finely chopped celery pieces.

variations

fried shrimp hosomaki

see base recipe page 133

fried asparagus hosomaki
Replace shrimp with 2 asparagus spears dipped in beaten egg before frying. Add a smear of chili mayonnaise (page 50).

fried burdock hosomaki
Replace shrimp with burdock as prepared on page 252. Fry for a little longer as burdock is quite tough. Roll with a little smoked paprika mayonnaise (page 50).

fried cod hosomaki
Prepare basic recipe, replacing shrimp with a thin strip of cod, about 3/4 oz.

fried avocado hosomaki
Replace shrimp with 2 pieces of avocado 1/3 in. wide and 2 3/4 in. long. Roll with smoked paprika mayonnaise (page 50).

fried sweet potato hosomaki
Replace shrimp with 2 pieces of sweet potato 1/3 in. wide and 2 3/4 in. long, thinly sliced and dipped in beaten egg before frying. Add a smear of chili mayonnaise (page 50).

fried zucchini hosomaki
Replace shrimp with 1 piece of zucchini, 1/3 in. wide and 6 in. long, dipped in beaten egg before frying. Add a smear of chili mayonnaise (page 50).

variations

tekkamaki – tuna hosomaki

see base recipe page 134

salmon hosomaki
Prepare the basic recipe, replacing tuna with a pencil-size strip of salmon.

squid, ume plum & cucumber hosomaki
Replace tuna with squid as prepared on page 17. Add julienned cucumber and a smear of ume plum paste.

bream & shiso hosomaki
Replace tuna with bream mixed with with torn leaves of shiso.

kabayaki faux eel & cucumber hosomaki
Replace tuna with faux eel as prepared on page 222, and roll with a pencil-size strip of cucumber.

crabstick & tobiko flying fish roe hosomaki
Replace tuna with crabsticks (sticks of surumi fish paste) sprinkled with flying fish roe.

yellowtail tempura hosomaki

see base recipe page 135

green bean tempura hosomaki
Prepare the basic recipe, replacing the yellowtail with raw green beans and sesame seeds.

scallop & mitsuba tempura hosomaki
Prepare the basic recipe, replacing the yellowtail with 1 large scallop cut in to pencil-thickness shapes, and add a sprinkle of mistuba trefoil leaf, or cilantro.

sea bass & yuzukosho tempura hosomaki
Prepare the basic recipe, replacing the yellowtail with 6-in. lengths of a fillet of sea bass, and a dab of yuzukosho paste before rolling.

futomaki

Futomaki are the large rolls that are particularly

popular in the West because they lend themselves

so amiably to interpretation and creativity;

essentially, you can mix and match flavors that

inspire you.

salmon & avocado futomaki

see variations page 172

Combining fish with vegetable is the most classic form of a futomaki, and the recipe below is probably most commonly found outside of Japan.

1 sheet nori
1/2 cup shari rice (page 28)
wasabi
1 oz. salmon fillet cut into two
    4 x 1/3-in. strips

1/2 large avocado cut into 4-in. strips
1 tsp. tobiko flying fish roe

Make the roll as described on pages 22–23.

Makes 1 roll, or 6–8 pieces

crispy salmon skin futomaki

see variations page 173

You won't find much cooked fish in a traditional sushi bar, but at home when you are making picnic food or a bento box for school lunch, cooked fish plays a larger role, as it often require less skill (oddly!) and stays fresh longer. In the spirit of appreciating nature's gifts and its finite resources, the skin of the salmon is surely worthy of a better end than the garbage can. Not only is it truly delicious when crisped under a broiler but it is highly nutritious, as most of the omega 3 and 6 and other minerals and vitamins are found in the fatty area just under the skin.

1 1/2 oz. salmon skin (try to leave about
   1/4 in. of salmon flesh under the skin)
sea salt
1 tbsp. teriyaki sauce (page 36)
1 sheet nori

1/2 cup shari rice (page 28)
a few leaves of lettuce
2 tsp. finely chopped scallion
1 tsp. of wasabi–tobiko flying fish roe (optional)

Cover the salmon skin pieces lightly with sea salt on both sides, and place under a broiler until they are crispy brown and the skin starts to bubble and darken. Set aside to cool. It should now feel nearly brittle. Cut the salmon skin into long lengths and brush with the teriyaki sauce. Make the futomaki roll with the lettuce and scallion as described on pages 22–23.

Makes 1 roll, or 6–8 pieces

california crab, flying fish roe & avocado uramaki

see variations page 174

Uramaki rolls are made by wrapping the roll with the nori on the inside. This opens up a large range of decorative options for garnish on the rice outside. Here we use flying fish roe, but you can use different roes.

1 tbsp. fresh crabmeat
1/2 sheet nori
1/2 cup shari rice (page 28)

wasabi
1/2 large avocado cut into 4-in. strips
1 tsp. tobiko red flying fish roe

For the crabmeat, a ratio of 2:1 white to brown meat is nice, but if you prefer it to taste more creamy, then reduce the white meat and add more brown meat. Make the uramaki roll with crabmeat and avocado as described on pages 24–25.

Shape into triangle shapes and arrange in a circle.

Makes 1 roll, or 6–8 pieces

panfried beef & teriyaki mustard sauce uramaki

see variations page 175

Panfrying a whole roll is another unconventional but delicious way to prepare sushi.

1 tsp. whole grain mustard
2 tbsp. teriyaki sauce (page 36)
butter for frying
1 tsp. scallion, cut into long diagonal slices
1 tbsp. green beans
1/2 sheet nori
1/2 cup shari rice (page 28)

1 tsp. julienned carrot
2 red chiles, cut in half and deseeded, julienned
   into thin slices
3 tbsp. fillet of sirloin beef
sea salt and black pepper
chopped chives

Mix the whole grain mustard with the teriyaki sauce and set aside. Heat the butter in a pan and panfry the scallion and green beans very lightly (or not at all if you prefer your greens crunchier). Make your uramaki with the green beans, scallion, julienned carrots, and lengths of red chile as described on pages 24–25. Cut the fillet of beef into long, thin slices; ideally each should be about 4 in. in length. Arrange the slices of beef, overlapping slightly, over and around the uramaki. Sprinkle with salt and pepper. Using the same butter used to fry the green beans and scallions, place the whole beef uramaki into the pan and fry to gently brown the beef. Add the teriyaki mustard sauce to the pan and fry for another minute. Remove the uramaki from the pan and reduce the teriyaki sauce. Wrap the beef uramaki like a sausage in a piece of plastic wrap and tighten at both ends to compress and shape the roll. Cut into 6 or 8 pieces and then remove the plastic wrap. Spoon a little of the reduced teriyaki mustard sauce over the pieces and top with chives.

Makes 1 roll, or 6–8 pieces

squid & mizuna wrapped in cucumber

see variations page 176

Another eye-catching method of rolling sushi is to wrap it in something other than nori. In this example we use cucumber, and the variations focus on crustaceans, cephalopods and mollusks.

4-in. length of large cucumber
1 sheet nori
1/2 cup shari rice (page 28)
wasabi
1 tsp. mentaiko chili pollock roe

1 oz. very fresh squid, cleaned and cut into
    julienne strips
2 tsp. carrot, julienned
2 tsp. mizuna leaves, washed and dried (use
    arugula if you can't find mizuna)

With a 6-in. knife, firmly hold the cucumber against the knife and turn the cucumber gradually to produce one long, uniform strip. If this is too difficult (and it is quite a skill!) it is all right to leave the roll unwrapped.

For this style, use the futomaki rolling technique as described on pages 22–23. Using a teaspoon, smear on the mentaiko chili pollock roe (if you can't find this in the Japanese grocery, substitute with a dab of wasabi and tobiko flying fish roe). Arrange the julienned strips of squid, carrot, and mizuna leaves. Continue rolling, but before you cut the roll, place it on top of the cucumber strip and wrap the roll once more in the cucumber. Trim the roll and cut into 6–8 pieces.

Makes 1 roll, or 6–8 pieces

softshell crab daikon wrap

see variations page 177

Lightly fried maki rolls are not traditional in Japan but have really taken hold in the West. They are best served as soon as you've made them so as to get that rare contrast in sushi between hot and cold in your mouth.

1 straight, uniform width daikon radish,
    trimmed and peeled
1 sheet nori
1/2 cup shari rice (page 28)
wasabi
2 tsp. tobiko red flying fish roe
chives cut into 4-in. lengths

1/2 large avocado cut into 4-in. strips
vegetable oil, for frying
1 soft shell crab
potato flour
1 tsp. chili mayonnaise, plus extra
    to serve (page 50)

Get the hard part out of the way and start with making the daikon peel. With a 6-in. knife, firmly hold the daikon against the knife and turn the daikon gradually to produce one long, uniform strip, or use a wide vegetable peeler to peel long strips. Roll the futomaki as described on pages 22–23. Add an unbroken smear of wasabi. Using a teaspoon, spread on the flying fish roe and add the long chives and avocado on top.

Bring about 1 in. of good vegetable oil in a small saucepan to 400°F. Dust the softshell crab with potato flour and deep fry for 3 to 4 minutes. Drain and squash the crab to compress it sufficiently for it to fit snugly in the roll. Add the crab to the roll while it is still hot. Continue rolling. Before cutting the roll, place it on top of the daikon strip and wrap the roll in the daikon. Trim the roll and cut into 6 or 8 pieces. Serve with chili mayonnaise.

Makes 1 roll, or 6–8 pieces

tempura shishito pepper futomaki

see variations page 178

This futomaki is all about texture — the crunchiness of the pepper tempura is a contrast to the softness of the warm cheese. This is one of the those dishes best served just as soon as it is made.

8–12 shishito (or Spanish pedron) peppers
2 oz. Gruyère cheese
black pepper
chopped chives
4 sheets nori
1 lb. shari rice (page 28)

1 cup all-purpose flour, plus a little extra
   for coating
1 large egg
1 1/2 cups ice water and ice cubes
vegetable oil, for deep-frying
4 tsp. runny honey

Wash and cut the tops off the shishito peppers. Reserve the tops. Sprinkle the cheese with black pepper and chopped chives and gently press the Gruyère into each pepper. Put the top of the pepper back on and secure with a toothpick. Make the futomaki as described on pages 22–23. Now make the tempura batter. The secret is not to beat the batter too vigorously, so mix the flour, egg, and ice water with chopsticks, leaving lumps of flour unblended. You can also add ice cubes if you like. Heat the vegetable oil in a small deep pan to 350°F. Or you can test the temperature by flicking in a drop of batter. It should sink and then rise: if it just sinks it is too cool, and if it rises right away it is too hot. Coat the shishito in a little flour and shake off the excess. Dip the shishito into the batter, then toss gently into the hot oil for about 3 minutes, or until the batter has turned golden. Remove the shishito with a stainless steel mesh spoon and drain on a wire rack or paper towels. Add the shishito to the roll while it is still hot, and drizzle a little honey over the top. Continue rolling and cut into 6 pieces.

Makes 4 rolls, or 24 pieces

avocado & ume plum uramaki

see variations page 179

Futomaki rolls can be one of those rare treats for vegetarians tired of never-ending goat cheese and hummus. The flavors of Japan make welcome changes as they are often unique.

1/2 sheet nori
1/2 cup shari rice (page 28)
shiso cress or chopped chives
1 tsp. ume plum paste

1/2 large avocado cut into 4-in. strips
lettuce leaves
1/2 oz. nimono daikon cut into 4-in. lengths

Make the uramaki roll as described on pages 24–25, sprinkling the outside of the roll with shiso cress or chopped chives.

Spread the ume plum paste along the middle of the roll, add the avocado, lettuce, and nimono daikon, and continue rolling.

Makes 1 roll, or 6–8 pieces

toasted tofu futomaki

see variations page 180

Smoky flavors work well in vegetable rolls. While tofu is not commonly found in sushi, as a vegetarian variation it is too tasty to miss.

marinade
3/4 cup soy sauce
1/2 cup mirin
1/2 cup rice vinegar

7 oz. firm tofu
2 whole shiitake mushrooms

1/2 red pepper
1 nori sheet
1/2 cup shari rice (page 28)
black pepper
1 tsp. scallion, chopped
1 tsp. ponzu sauce (page 39)

Bring the soy, mirin, and vinegar gently to a boil, remove from heat and let cool.

Drain the tofu and slice into 1/3-in. x 4-in. blocks. Cut the shiitake in half. Cut the red pepper into thick long slices. Place the tofu together with the red pepper and shiitake mushrooms in the cooled marinade and soak for 30–40 minutes in the refrigerator.

Drain and place the tofu, mushrooms, and pepper on a charcoal grill. Grill until lightly browned. The tofu will take the longest.

Make your futomaki as described on pages 22–23, sprinkling the red pepper, shiitake, and tofu with black pepper and scallion. Dip the rolls in ponzu citrus soy to eat.

Makes 1 roll, or 6–8 pieces

honey & soy quail with fig & cucumber futomaki

see variations page 181

Far from conventional, this is a delicious example of just how far you can take sushi away from its roots.

1 large quail breast

marinade
1 cup soy sauce
1 cup concentrated apple juice
1 cup sake
4 tsp. oroshi grated ginger with its juice

vegetable oil, for frying
2 figs, stems removed
2 nori sheets
1 cup shari rice (page 28)
1 oz. julienned cucumber
Japanese mustard

Debone and trim the quail breast. Place the quail in a colander and pour hot water over it. Rinse in cold water and set aside. Make the marinade of soy, apple juice, sake, and ginger and pour half of it over the quail in a flat-bottomed bowl and marinate for at least 30 minutes (overnight is okay, too) in the refrigerator. Reserve the remaining half of the marinade. Heat the oil in a skillet, remove the quail from the marinade, and panfry for a minute. Add a little of the reserved marinade and continue to cook on each side for another 2–3 minutes (or longer if you prefer your quail not to be pink inside). Remove from the pan and cut the quail into 4-in. slices. Cut the figs in quarters. Make your futomaki as described on pages 22–23, wrapping the quail, fig, and cucumber. Add on top a teaspoon of the juices left in the pan and serve with Japanese mustard.

Makes 2 rolls, or 12 pieces

seared beef uramaki

see variations page 182

Another unconventional maki, visually stunning with the sushi roll wrapped in a tunnel of seared beef tataki.

vegetable oil, for frying
4 oz. fillet of wagyu (or sirloin beef)
1/2 cup sake
1/2 cup dark soy sauce
1 asparagus stem
1/2 sheet nori
1/2 cup shari rice (page 28)

Japanese mustard (comparable English or
American mustard will do)
wasabi mayonnaise (page 50)
2 tsp. butter
2 tsp. finely sliced scallion or red onion
black pepper

Heat the oil in a heavy-bottomed pan and sear the beef until brown, about 1–2 minutes on each side. Place the seared beef in a bowl of ice water and leave for about 5 minutes. Remove and drain. The surface of the beef should be nicely browned, while the inside should be raw. Combine the sake and soy in a flat-bottomed bowl and marinate the beef for at least 30 minutes, or overnight if you prefer, in the refrigerator. Steam the asparagus in a colander over a saucepan of boiling water, lid on, for a minute or so, making sure it is still firm and crunchy. Remove and cool. Make the uramaki as described on pages 24–25. When flipping over the nori, smear a dab of Japanese mustard down the center of the nori instead of wasabi. Arrange the asparagus over it and roll. Cut the marinated beef into very thin slices. On a separate piece of plastic-wrapped bamboo mat, arrange the beef slices to cover the nori sheet. Place the asparagus maki roll on top of the beef and roll again. Starting from the middle, cut into 6 equal pieces. Once cut, remove the plastic wrap from each piece. Drizzle with wasabi mayonnaise and top with thinly sliced scallion or red onion.

Makes 1 roll, or 6 pieces

seared duck & grapefruit uramaki

see variations page 183

Topping a futomaki roll with a slice of seared meat makes an attractive dish, and the texture is succulent with the seared duck and firmness of the grapefruit.

marinade
3/4 cup rice vinegar
2 tbsp. honey
6 tbsp. mirin
1 3/4 cups dark soy sauce

4 oz. duck breast
1/2 grapefruit

1 oz. cucumber, julienned
1/2 sheet nori
1/2 cup shari rice (page 28)
chopped chives
Japanese mustard (comparable English or
    American mustard will do)
2 tsp. finely sliced scallion or red onion
red chile

Trim the duck breast. Combine the vinegar, honey, mirin, and soy in a flat-bottomed bowl and use half of this mixture to marinate the duck for at least 30 minutes in the refrigerator. Remove from the marinade. Heat a pan and fry the duck breast, skin-side down, for a minute or so and turn to brown the other side. Remove from the heat and wrap in aluminum foil for 10 minutes. The outside should be crispy brown while the inside is less well cooked. Pour the remaining, unused marinade into the pan with the duck juices and reduce over medium heat. Set aside and cool. Cut the grapefruit into long segments. Make the nori and shari rice following the description for uramaki on pages 24–25, with the chives on the outside of the roll. When flipped over, add a dab of Japanese mustard (instead of the wasabi) down the center of the nori. Arrange the grapefruit and cucumber over it and roll. Starting from the middle, cut into 6 equal pieces. Remove the marinated duck from the foil and cut into thin slices. Place a slice of duck on top of each piece of maki. Decorate with thinly sliced scallion or red onion and red chile, and spoon over a little of the reduced marinade.

Makes 1 roll, or 6 pieces

poached sea bass with katsuo boshi & yuzukosho uramaki

see variations page 184

I've chosen to use sea bass here, but you can use any sustainably caught fish that is local to your waters. Even the fish that are traditionally not used in raw sushi such as pollock or cod can be used here, as the fish is to be cooked.

1 1/2 oz. sea bass fillet
7 fl. oz. soy sauce
3 fl. oz. rice vinegar
3 fl. oz. mirin
1/2 sheet nori

1/2 cup shari rice (page 28)
a dab of yuzukosho
1 tsp. mizuna
1 tsp. katsuo boshi

Place the sea bass in a small ovenproof dish. Combine the soy, vinegar, and mirin and pour over the sea bass. Poach in the oven, pre-heated to 350°F for about 10–15 minutes, depending on the thickness of the fillet.

When cool, shred the fillet into small pieces. Make the nori and shari rice following the description for uramaki on pages 24–25, dabbing a little yuzukosho on it instead of wasabi and filling the center with shredded poached sea bass and mizuna leaves. Roll the finished uramaki in katsuo boshi flakes and cut into 6 pieces.

Katuso boshi looses its flaky texture very quickly when exposed to anything wet, so it is best to leave this last step to when you are ready to eat it.

Makes 1 roll, or 6 pieces

"sea chicken" tuna salad futomaki

see variations page 185

The taste of canned tuna is so different from that of a freshly cut piece of maguro (the red meat of the yellowfin, big eye, or bluefin tuna), that the Japanese refer to it as sea chicken. Traditionally, fishermen have referred to the white meat of the albacore tuna as chicken of the sea, but more recently skipjack tuna is the favored tuna species in a can.

1 oz. canned tuna in water
1 tsp. finely chopped onion
1 tsp. red radish, sliced
1 sheet nori

1/2 cup shari rice (page 28)
wasabi
2 tsp. watercress

Drain the canned tuna and combine with the onion and red radish. Make the futomaki roll with the tuna mix and watercress sprigs as described on pages 22–23.

Makes 1 roll, or 6 pieces

dragon roll shrimp, salmon & avocado uramaki

see variations page 186

This recipe is inspired by the Chinese dragon boats. Although the shrimp head might seem overly commanding, once you get past the peering eyes, it is actually really tasty! They are, of course, totally optional.

2 large tiger shrimp
potato flour
vegetable oil, for frying
1 1/2 oz. salmon fillet

1/2 avocado
1/2 sheet nori
1/2 cup shari rice (page 28)
chili mayonnaise (page 50)

Peel the shrimp, removing the heads but being careful to leave the tails in place. Reserve the heads. To make the shrimp flat, turn it onto its back and make 3 small incisions at even intervals along its center, making sure not to cut through to the other side. Then turn the shrimp onto its tummy and press gently along its spine to stretch it out a little more. Rinse, coat with potato flour, and deep-fry in a small skillet of hot oil. Drain on paper towels. Cut the salmon into 4 thin slices. Cut the avocado lengthways into thin slices.

Make the uramaki as described on pages 24–25, placing the shrimp in the middle, with the tail popping out at the side. Arrange alternate slices of avocado and salmon slices over the uramaki. Place a piece of plastic wrap over the top of the salmon and avocado and press gently into shape. Cut into 6 equal pieces and, once cut, remove the plastic wrap. Decorate with the shrimp heads and chili mayonnaise.

Makes 1 roll, or 6 pieces

stained glass window futomaki

see variations page 187

This maki looks tremendous, and once you've got the hang of it, isn't as hard as it looks.

1/2 cup shari rice (page 28)
1 oz. yellow masago capelin roe
1 oz. wasabi masago green capelin roe
1 oz. red tobiko flying fish roe or masago
  capelin roe

2 sheets nori, cut in to halves
1/2 oz. tamago omelet (page 189) cut into
  a 3-in. pencil shape

To begin, it is a good idea to think through what you need to do to create the effect shown in the photograph: rolls are wrapped inside one another, then cut into quarters, turned over so that the cut square edges are on the outside and curved ones on the inside, then re-shaped into one large, square maki. Use far less rice in each of the maki than you would normally use.

Divide the rice into 3 and mix each with a different-colored roe. It is best to use masago capelin roe, as the eggs are slightly smaller. Next make the smallest, inner maki roll. Cut one half of the nori sheet into half again, and use one of the quarters. With the shortest edge nearest you, spread a thin layer of yellow masago rice evenly over the nori, then roll like a hosomaki, so that the edges of the nori only just meet, and don't overlap.

Then take a 1/2 sheet of nori and with the shortest side nearest you, spread over a thin layer of green masago rice, leaving about 1/4 of the nori uncovered at the top, place the yellow roll on top of the green rice and roll like a hosomaki. Once rolled, cut off the uncovered nori that is sticking out.

Take the last piece of 1/2 of nori, and with the shortest side facing, cover evenly with a thin layer of orange rice leaving a 1/2-in. gap at the top. Place the yellow-green double roll on top of the orange rice, and roll. You should now have a colorful futomaki roll.

Leave it to set for at least 10 minutes. Then, with a sharp long knife, cut the three-color futomaki roll in half, lengthways. Cut each half once more lengthways so as to make 4 long quarters. Take two quarters and flip them over so the curve edge is on the inside and the square edge on the outside. Place the piece of tamago in the center of the curves. Complete the square by adding the remaining two quarters. Place the whole square roll on top of a 1/2 sheet of nori and roll one more time, to encase the inside. Gently use the bamboo mat to shape the square. Remove the mat and cut into 4-6 pieces to display your elaborate center!

Makes 1 roll, or 4-6 pieces

variations

salmon & avocado futomaki

see base recipe page 145

negitoro tuna belly & scallion futomaki
Replace salmon with yellowfin or big eye tuna fillet, chopped finely almost to a paste. Mix in a touch of wasabi mayonnaise (page 50) and finely chopped scallions.

spicy tuna & shichimi 7-spice pepper futomaki
Prepare the basic recipe, replacing salmon with 4-in. strips of tuna, and avocado with julienned strips of cucumber and iceberg lettuce. Sprinkle over shichimi pepper and roll.

bream, ume plum & cucumber futomaki
Prepare the basic recipe, replacing salmon with 4-in. strips of bream, and avocado with julienned strips of cucumber and frisse lettuce leaves. Replace wasabi with ume plum paste.

lemon sole & shiso futomaki
Prepare the basic recipe, replacing salmon with 4-in. strips of lemon sole. To avocado, add a few leaves of endive and shiso.

yellowtail tuna & spicy daikon radish futomaki
Prepare the basic recipe, replacing salmon with 4-in. strips of yellowtail tuna, and avocado with 1 teaspoon daikon radish with finely chopped chile, strips of cucumber, and shichimi.

crispy salmon skin futomaki

see base recipe page 146

tuna & corn futomaki

Drain a can of tuna (5 oz.) and mix with 3 1/2 oz. corn and a level tablespoon of wasabi mayonnaise (page 50). Make the futomaki roll with the tuna mixture, thinly sliced red radish, and sprigs of watercress.

poached salmon, asparagus & wasabi mayonnaise futomaki

Poach a few small pieces of salmon, steam a stem of asparagus, and roll the futomaki with a dab of wasabi mayonnaise (page 50).

poached salmon, cucumber & watercress futomaki

Poach a few small pieces of salmon and roll the futomaki with julienned strips of cucumber and a sprig of watercress.

katsu deep-fried salmon & fennel futomaki

Breadcrumb and deep-fry some salmon pieces (page 234). Roll with julienned strips of fennel, a few leaves of iceberg lettuce, and a dab of tonkatsu mayonnaise (page 50).

kabayaki faux eel & cucumber futomaki

Repace salmon with kabayaki faux eel (as prepared on page 222). Roll with julienned slices of cucumber. Best eaten when the faux eel is still a little warm from broiling.

california crab, flying fish roe & avocado uramaki

see base recipe page 149

tiger shrimp & avocado uramaki
Replace crabmeat with 2 tiger shrimp and replace roe with finely chopped chives.

lobster & avocado uramaki
Replace crabmeat with lobster as prepared on page 62.

scallop & avocado uramaki
Replace crabmeat with 1 large raw scallop, and replace roe with finely chopped mitsuba leaves. Roll with the avocado and a few leaves of lettuce.

tiger shrimp & okra uramaki
Replace crabmeat with 2 large tiger shrimp mixed with nimono-style (simmered) okra (page 73) and replace roe with sesame seeds.

squid with ume plum, shiso & caviar uramaki
Replace crabmeat with julienned strips of raw squid meat as prepared on page 17. Replace roe with caviar, and roll using a smear of ume plum and a scatter of torn shiso leaves.

tiger shrimp, salmon, cream cheese & avocado uramaki
Replace crabmeat with 1 tiger shrimp and 1 tablespoon of salmon, a smear of cream cheese, and a sprinkle of chopped chives. Replace roe with black sesame seeds.

panfried beef & teriyaki mustard sauce uramaki

see base recipe page 150

panfried duck, green beans, carrot, chile & scallions uramaki
Prepare the basic recipe, replacing beef with slices of duck.

panfried beef, asparagus, burdock, chile & watercress uramaki
Prepare the basic recipe, replacing green beans with asparagus and the carrot with kinpira burdock (page 252). Use watercress to add sharpness instead of scallion.

panfried tuna, green beans, carrot, chile & scallion uramaki
Prepare the basic recipe, replacing beef with 1/4-in. thick slices of tuna.

panfried duck, green beans, daikon radish, sesame seeds & scallion uramaki
Prepare the basic recipe, replacing beef with duck. Add julienned daikon instead of carrot and sesame seeds instead of chile.

panfried tuna with wasabi mayonnaise uramaki
Prepare the basic recipe, replacing beef with 1/4-in. thick slices of tuna, replace the green beans with cos lettuce, spread with a little wasabi mayonnaise.

panfried duck, cucumber, scallion & carrot with hoisin sauce uramaki
Prepare the basic recipe, replacing beef with duck. Add julienned cucumber and scallion along with the carrot and spread a little hoisin sauce.

variations

squid & mizuna wrapped in cucumber

see base recipe page 152

octopus, cucumber & scallion futomaki wrap
Replace squid with boiled octopus as prepared on page 74. Add long strips of cucumber and chopped scallion to the roll. Wrap with a film of daikon radish.

tiger shrimp, green beans & smoked paprika mayonnaise futomaki wrap
Replace squid with shrimp as prepared on page 225. Roll with 1/3 oz. blanched green beans and add a teaspoon of smoked paprika mayonnaise (page 50), wrap with cucumber.

scallop & shiso futomaki wrap
Replace squid with raw scallops as prepared on page 110. Add some torn shiso leaves to the roll. Add a teaspoon of ponzu sauce and wrap in cucumber.

lobster & yuzu mayonnaise futomaki wrap
Replace squid with lobster as prepared on page 62. Add lettuce leaves and a teaspoon of yuzu mayonnaise (page 34) and wrap with cucumber.

tiger shrimp & yuba with sweet chili mayonnaise futomaki wrap
Replace squid with shrimp as prepared on page 225. Pat dry 2 strips of yuba tofu skin strips, which in the standard form are around 2 x 3 in. Spoon over a teaspoon of sweet chili mayonnaise and wrap in radish.

variations

softshell crab daikon wrap

see base recipe page 154

shrimp, avocado & chili mayonnaise futomaki wrap
Replace crabmeat with 2 fried tiger shrimp and roll with avocado, fish roe, and lettuce.

lobster, avocado, wasabi mayonnaise & caviar futomaki wrap
Replace crabmeat with 7 oz. fried lobster meat. Roll with cos lettuce, a sprinkle of shiso cress or mustard and cress, a teaspoon of wasabi mayonnaise and a teaspoon of sustainably raised caviar or black flying fish roe.

squid, mizuna, chile, sea salt & lime futomaki wrap
Replace crabmeat with 7 oz. raw squid cut into even pieces. Roll with mizuna, chopped red chiles, zest of lime, and a sprinkle of sea salt.

oyster & yuzu mayonnaise futomaki wrap
Replace crabmeat with 2 fried oysters. Roll with lettuce and a teaspoon of yuzu mayonnaise (page 34).

variations

tempura shishito pepper futomaki

See base recipe page 156

pumpkin–burdock tempura & sesame dressing futomaki
Replace pepper with 2 oz. pumpkin and 2 oz. burdock, each cut into 1/3-in. thick slices. Add a little iceberg lettuce and evenly spread a teaspoon of sesame dressing (page 53) over the vegetables before rolling.

avocado & smoked paprika mayonnaise futomaki
Replace pepper with avocado and add a teaspoon of smoked paprika mayonnaise (page 50) before rolling the maki.

zucchini flower, burrata cheese & honey futomaki
Stuff a zucchini flower with burrata cheese and complete the roll with black pepper and honey.

shishito pepper stuffed with gorgonzola cheese & honey futomaki
Stuff the shishito pepper with Gorgonozola cheese and complete the roll with a sprinkle of toasted hazelnuts and honey.

variations

avocado & ume plum uramaki

see base recipe page 157

shiso & cucumber uramaki
Omit avocado and roll with shiso leaf, torn with your fingers, julienned strips of daikon and cucumber, and a couple of lettuce leaves. Replace shiso cress with chopped parsley.

pickled ginger, avocado & red pepper uramaki
Prepare the basic recipe, adding pickled ginger (page 32), 4-in. strips of red pepper, julienned carrot and cucumber, lettuce leaves, and a sprinkle of sesame seed. Use chopped chives on the outside.

burdock & carrot uramaki
Omit daikon and avocado, and roll using the recipe on page 252. Use sesame seeds on the outside.

purple sprouting broccoli & sesame uramaki
Omit daikon and avocado, and roll with a couple of sprigs purple sprouting broccoli, blanched, a teaspoon of sesame dressing (page 53), raw spinach leaves, and julienned carrot.

toasted tofu futomaki

see base recipe page 158

toasted tofu & cucumber futomaki
Prepare the basic recipe, and roll with julienned cucumber and a sprinkle of sesame seeds.

toasted tofu, sunblush tomato, pine nuts & basil futomaki
Prepare the basic recipe, and add a couple of sunblush tomatoes, with some cut in half, a few pine nuts, and some torn leaves of basil. Serve with yuzu mayonnaise (page 34).

tamago sweet omelet, shiitake mushroom, bamboo shoot & watercress futomaki
Prepare the basic recipe, omitting red pepper and replacing tofu with shiitake and pickled calabash (page 49). Add to the roll a 4-in. slice of the sweet omelet, strips of bamboo shoot (either from a can or vacuum packed) washed and drained well, and some watercress leaves.

tamago sweet omelet, carrot, green bean & inari futomaki
Prepare the basic recipe, replacing tofu with green bean and carrot. Add to the roll strips of tamago omelet and inari tofu (fried tofu skin), sprinkle with sesame seeds.

enoki mushroom, tamago sweet omelet, mizuna & yuba futomaki
Prepare the basic recipe, replacing tofu with enoki mushrooms and lightly broil. Add to the roll a strip of yuba tofu skin, tamago sweet omelet, and a few mizuna leaves.

honey & soy quail with fig & cucumber futomaki

see base recipe page 161

seared quail & chestnut futomaki
Prepare the basic recipe, adding pieces of boiled chestnut to the pan while frying the quail. Roll with julienned cucumber.

seared duck, scallion & red chile futomaki
Prepare the basic recipe, replacing quail with duck breast. Roll with julienned cucumber, chopped scallion, julienned carrots, and chopped red chile.

panfried chorizo & green & yellow pepper futomaki
Replace quail with chorizo, cut into 4-in. lengths and halved. Omit figs, and cucumbers. Make marinade, but omit marinating stage. Cut a green and yellow pepper into long slices and fry briefly in the marinade sauce with the chorizo. Serve with smoked paprika mayonnaise (page 50).

gyoza dumplings, mizuna & daikon futomaki
Gyoza — pork and cabbage dumplings — can be found in most Japanese grocery stores. Steam the gyoza. Omit the marinating stage. Add a drop of marinade sauce to a skillet and panfry the gyoza for a couple of minutes. Roll with mizuna and julienned daikon.

variations

seared beef uramaki

see base recipe page 162

kabayaki faux eel, cucumber & avocado uramaki

Make the faux eel using the recipe on page 222. Make the inside roll using the faux eel and julienned cucumber. Make the outside wrap with finely sliced avocado. Spoon over a little faux eel sauce and top with pink peppercorn.

foie gras poached nashi pear, umeshu plum wine & cucumber uramaki

Cut 3 oz. foie gras liver into 3/4-in. thick slices. Coat with potato flour, fry until golden brown, and drain on paper towels. Mix together equal parts of soy, rice vinegar, and umeshu plum wine to the pan and heat over high heat. Add 1 nashi pear and poach until soft but still crunchy. Remove pear and reduce remaining liquid. Add splash of white truffle oil and a few pink peppercorns. Roll with the foie gras and nashi pear on the inside. Make the outside using thinly sliced cucumber. Cut and top with fried leeks and a little remaining liquid.

halloumi cheese, grilled shishito pepper & pancetta uramaki

Omit beef, asparagus, and wasabi mayonnaise. Brush 1/2 oz. each halloumi and pepper, cut into 4-in. strips, with a mixture of soy and sake and broil. Roll using halloumi and pepper on the inside and pancetta slices on the outside.

mozzarella & smoked salmon uramaki

Omit beef, asparagus, and wasabi mayonnaise. Roll using mozzarella, chopped chives, and lettuce leaves on the inside and slices of smoked salmon on the outside.

variations

seared duck & grapefruit uramaki

see base recipe page 164

beef, fig & green bean uramaki
Prepare the basic recipe, replacing duck with marinated beef fillet. Assemble the inside of the uramaki with blanched green beans and slices of raw fig, and the outside with chopped chives. Top each piece of maki with a slice of seared beef and some thinly sliced onions.

chicken, yuzukosho & spinach uramaki
Prepare the basic recipe, replacing duck with marinated thigh of chicken. Make the inside roll with a dab of yuzukosho and spinach leaves, and the outside with shiso cress. Top each piece of maki with a slice of the chicken, and decorate with shiso cress or mustard and cress.

gammon, pineapple & cress uramaki
Prepare the basic recipe, replacing duck with a marinated piece of gammon. Make the inside roll with pineapple and cucumber, and the outside with shiso cress or mustard and cress. Top each piece of maki with a slice of gammon, and sprinkle with black pepper and finely sliced red chile.

variations

poached sea bass with katsuo boshi & yuzukosho uramaki

see base recipe page 166

cod, mizuna & katsuo boshi uramaki
Replace sea bass with cod or any sustainably caught local whitefish available to you.

tuna, cucumber & spicy flying fish roe uramaki
Replace sea bass with tuna, and mizuna with cucumber. Substitute the outside katsuo boshi for a mixture of flying fish roe and shichimi pepper.

shellfish mix with mizuna & katsuboshi uramaki
Replace sea bass with a mixture of shellfish — clams, scallops, mussels, and oysters.

smoked haddock, mizuna & prosciutto uramaki
Replace sea bass with smoked haddock. Substitute the outside katsuo boshi for flecks of chopped prosciutto ham.

poached monkfish, cucumber & prosciutto uramaki
Replace sea bass with poached monkfish, and mizuna with cucumber. Substitute the outside katsuo boshi for flecks of chopped prosciutto ham.

variations

"sea chicken" tuna salad futomaki

see base recipe page 168

sea chicken tuna salad & corn futomaki
Replace red radish and watercress with corn.

sea chicken tuna salad & tomato futomaki
Replace red radish and watercress with chopped tomato.

sea chicken tuna salad & jalapeño futomaki
Replace red radish, onion, and watercress with chopped jalapeño.

sea chicken tuna salad, red kidney beans & green pepper futomaki
Replace red radish, onion, and watercress with kidney beans and chopped green pepper.

sea chicken tuna salad & black olive futomaki
Replace red radish, onion, and watercress with chopped black olives.

dragon roll shrimp, salmon & avocado uramaki

see base recipe page 169

faux eel, salmon & avocado dragon roll
Replace shrimp with faux eel, as prepared on page 222.

shrimp & avocado dragon roll
Butterfly the shrimp to make a wider shape. Make the inside roll using julienned carrot and lettuce. Wrap with slices of avocado and boiled shrimp.

tuna & avocado dragon roll
Make the inside roll using julienned carrot and lettuce, and wrap with slices of avocado and tuna.

faux eel, cucumber & avocado dragon roll
Replace shrimp with faux eel, as prepared on page 222 and wrap with varying shades of green using thinly sliced avocado and cucumber.

tuna & avocado dragon roll
Make the inside roll using watercress and prawn, and wrap with slices of avocado and tuna.

variations

stained glass window futomaki

see base recipe page 170

soboro stained glass window futomaki
Prepare the basic recipe, replacing roe with a ground meat or fish called "soboro." You can buy this in Japanese supermarkets, but beware, often they are just sugar and color additives. Replace the tamago with your favorite white fish.

salmon & caviar stained glass window futomaki
Prepare the basic recipe, making the three different-colored rice using caviar or black herring roe, plain white rice, and green masago with a band of bright orange raw or smoked salmon.

saintly vegetarian stained glass window futomaki
Prepare the basic recipe, making the three different-colored rice using black sesame seeds, the purple of ume plum furikake seasoning (which can be purchased from most Japanese supermarkets) and finely chopped green shiso leaves mixed with the rice. Your center can be made with a band of green cucumber or yellow oshinko pickle.

sashimi

Sashimi, put simply, is freshly cut slices of uncooked fish, and it harnesses the natural good flavor of the ingredients. Although sushi looks simple, it is absolutely true that only those who possess good knife skills and understand the proper treatment of fish can create sashimi that has a fresh, superior taste. It is all quite subtle, but you will recognize it when you experience it.

tamago sweet omelet sashimi

see variations page 209

Sushi, being based on raw ingredients, has always been hazardous to the tummy, so some say that a sushi chef's skills should be tested on the quality of his tamago sweet omelet.

1 tsp. sugar	1 tbsp. mirin
2 fl. oz. dashi (page 44)	6 eggs
1 fl. oz. soy sauce	vegetable oil, for frying

Dissolve the sugar in the dashi, soy, and mirin. Lightly beat the eggs with a fork and combine them with the dashi mixture. Heat the pan (ideally a square one, as is conventional in Japan, though a round pan will suffice) and very lightly brush on the oil. Then pour 1/3 of the omelet mix onto the pan, tilting it back and forth so as to cover the base with a thin layer of egg. Cook on medium heat until the edges are a little crisp, but the middle remains soft and runny. Then, with chopsticks or a spatula, fold the omelet in half and then into a quarter, and move it to the edge of the pan. Next pour another 1/3 of the omelet mixture into the pan, lifting up the folded egg to allow the new egg mixture to run underneath it. Once cooked, this second omelet should be folded in half, then into a quarter, on top of the first, folded omelet. Repeat this process with the last 1/3 of the egg mixture, folding it for the last time. Remove this solid block of omelet from the pan and allow to cool before cutting. (If a round pan was used, trim off the round edges to make a square block of omelet.)

Tamago may be served as sashimi, with no rice and cut diagonally. Eat with soy sauce and perhaps a little daikon oroshi, grated radish.

Makes 3 portions

whitefish sashimi of red mullet, leeks & ginger oroshi

see variations page 210

Traditionally, whitefish such as sea bass and snapper were the prized fish to eat, with salmon becoming popular only with the advent of salmon farms in the 1990s, and tuna only since the 1920s. Before then it was considered only fit for cat food! Westernization of the Japanese diet perhaps can account for the recent enjoyment of fattier fish.

1 whole red mullet, weighing at least 1 3/4 lbs.
  (A smaller and therefore sexually immature
  fish should be avoided.)

7 oz. tsuma daikon white radish
5 tsp. grated ginger
5 tsp. finely chopped leek

Prepare the red mullet fillet as described on pages 16–17. To cut the fillet into sashimi slices, using a super-sharp knife, cut straight down across the grain, drawing the knife toward you. Start at the far end of the fillet and begin with the heel of the knife, drawing it down and upward as you cut through the flesh. The slices should be very thin and weigh about 1/3 of an oz. each. This is thinner than the cut for a softer fish such as salmon or tuna. Arrange the shredded daikon on a plate and stack up the sashimi slices on top of it. Using a teaspoon, dab a little of the grated ginger on top of every other slice of mullet and decorate with chopped leek.

Makes 1 portion

hamachi yellowtail sashimi, herb ceviche sauce & ponzu olive oil

see variations page 211

Softer, fattier fish like yellowtail can take the more robust, intense flavorings and sauces, and the creaminess of hamachi yellowtail goes well with this ceviche-style sashimi.

5 oz. hamachi yellowtail fillet
a small amount daikon tsuma (page 27)
1/2 cup ceviche sauce (page 43)
2 tsp. finely chopped flat parsley
2 tsp. finely chopped cilantro
1 tsp. grated oroshi daikon mixed with a drop
    of soy sauce

shiso cress
1 red jalapeño, cut into thin slices
2 tbsp. ponzu sauce (page 39)
2 tbsp. olive oil

Yellowtail are large fish, and you are unlikely to come across whole fish outside of Japan. Cut your yellowtail fillet into slices as described on page 18 of the introduction on cutting large fish. Combine the ceviche sauce with the finely chopped parsley and cilantro. Pour a little of this ceviche herb sauce on the center of the plate, and then arrange the shredded daikon directly on top of it. Arrange the fish slices as you like around the daikon. Top each slice of fish with a spot of grated oroshi daikon with soy, a leaf of shiso cress, and a thin slice of red jalapeño.

Mix the ponzu and olive oil together and drizzle over the yellowtail just before serving.

Makes 1 portion

marinated sashimi of mackerel, scallion & oroshi ginger

see variations page 212

When mackerel is in season (generally the warmer months in the northern hemisphere, and July to October in the southern hemisphere) the high oil content in the flesh means that it is quick to deteriorate. Because the flesh of the mackerel is tender and disintegrates easily, when filleting the fish try to cut it cleanly with as few knife strokes as possible. This will help keep the flesh from oxidization and the texture firm.

7 oz. marinated mackerel fillet (page 61)
7 oz. tsuma daikon white radish (page 27)
lemon slices

5 tsp. oroshi grated ginger
7 tbsp. chopped scallion
wasabi

Use the marinated mackerel as described on page 61. Arrange the tsuma daikon on a plate and ring the sashimi slices around the top of it. Insert a small slice of lemon between each slice of mackerel. Using a teaspoon, spoon a little ginger oroshi on top of every other slice of mackerel. Decorate with scallion, and serve with a dab of wasabi on the side.

Makes 1 portion

usuzukuri thinly sliced turbot, ponzu, oroshi daikon & shiso cress

see variations page 213

Flatfish are often finely sliced to showcase their translucent flesh and the fresh, firm texture. Usuzukuri is usually served with the classic citrus soy sauce, ponzu.

1 turbot
2 tsp. daikon oroshi grated white radish
3 tbsp. ponzu sauce (page 39)

4 tsp. shiso cress (most small leaves or sprouts work here)
1 lemon, cut into thin slices

You probably won't know how your turbot was caught, but try to choose a gill-netted or line-caught one, as a trawl-caught fish will have battered and bruised flesh. Ideally, your turbot will have been killed quickly and have had the blood drained out, providing reduced opportunity to contaminate the glassy white flesh.

Fillet the turbot as described on page 18 of the introduction for 5-piece filleting.

With a super-sharp knife, cut the fillet into paper-thin slices with the technique described on page 190; the idea is that they will be thin enough to see through. Once you have enough slices to fill a plate, arrange them as you like. Place the daikon oroshi on the overlapping fish slices and drizzle the ponzu sauce over the top of the grated radish. Sprinkle with shiso and decorate with lemon slices.

Serve the rest of the ponzu sauce in a small dipping bowl so that when eating you can pick up each "petal" and dip it lightly into the ponzu.

Makes 1 portion

aburi salmon sashimi ceviche & truffle olive oil

see variations page 214

Aburi simply means to scorch, and it is a technique used to firm up a fish on the outside. Traditionally this would have been achieved using a charcoal grill.

5 oz. salmon fillet
sea salt and black pepper
2 fl. oz. ceviche sauce (page 43)
2 tsp. daikon oroshi grated white radish
1 tsp. finely chopped chives

a splash of truffle oil
2 tbsp. olive oil
shiso cress or mustard and cress
daikon white radish curls

Cut the salmon fillet into slices as described on page 18 of the introduction on cutting large fish. Sprinkle the fillet with sea salt and black pepper. Blowtorch the fillet enough to lightly brown the surface. (Or panfry in butter if you don't have a blowtorch.)

Cut the salmon into 1/4-in. slices. Arrange them as you like on a serving dish. Combine the ceviche sauce with the grated white radish and chopped chives. Spoon a teaspoon of ceviche mixture on top of the salmon, followed by a splash of truffle oil. Truffle oil is very pungent, so use it sparingly. Drizzle the olive oil over the salmon just before serving. Decorate with shiso cress or mustard and cress, and daikon curls.

Makes 1 portion

sesame-encrusted salmon sashimi & spicy korean chili dressing

see variations page 215

Seared sashimi is a firm favorite in modern Japanese cooking, and the seared fattier fish are robust enough to support the strong flavor of a spicy chili dressing.

5 oz. salmon fillet
sea salt
black pepper
1 oz. mixed black and white sesame seeds

vegetable oil, for frying
1/2 cup Korean chili sauce (page 54)
1 oz. micro greens
shiso cress

Prepare the salmon fillet as described in the introduction on page 18. Rub the fillet with salt and black pepper. Roll in the sesame seeds so that the outside is fully coated. Heat the oil in a skillet and panfry the salmon for about one minute on each side. Remove from the heat.

When cool, slice the salmon into thick slices of about 3/4 oz. each. Pour the Korean chili sauce onto a serving plate. Arrange the salmon slices on top of the sauce, and decorate with micro greens and shiso cress.

Makes 1 portion

squid sashimi & ikura salmon roe

see variations page 216

The notion of eating raw cephalopods conjures up images of chewy, fishy, slimy things, but in fact, the opposite is true. Squid and octopus eaten raw taste of the sweetness of the sea, and their texture has a kind of crunch to the bite.

4 tsp. ikura salmon roe	5 oz. squid fillet
3 tbsp. sake	wasabi
3 tbsp. soy sauce	1 oz. of wakame and daikon tsuma (page 27)

Place the salmon roe in a small bowl and cover with the sake and soy. Leave in a refrigerator for at least 4 hours to marinate. Pour off the soy and sake, taking care not to break the eggs.

Prepare the whole squid as described on page 17. Place the squid fillet on a chopping board and slice into thin julienned strips. This cutting enhances the texture when in the mouth. Arrange the julienned squid on a plate, top with a teaspoon of salmon roe. Serve with wakame and daikon tsuma and, in a seperate dish, a little wasabi mixed with soy sauce.

Alternatively, you can make a roll of squid with something colorful such as cucumber or a shiso leaf. Prepare a 4-in. square fillet of squid, and make diagonal scores on one side of the flesh, taking care not to cut through it. With a 6-in. knife, firmly hold a 4-in. length of cucumber against the knife and turn the cucumber gradually to produce one long, uniform strip. Cover the squid with the unbroken strip of cucumber, and roll as you might a maki. Cut into 3/4-in.-wide slices.

Makes 1 portion

octopus sashimi, teriyaki & sesame

see variations page 217

Sashimi usually denotes raw fish, but cooked octopus, squid, shrimp, or scallops can be made into sashimi-style dishes.

5 oz. octopus tentacle ends
1 1/2 oz. julienned cucumber
2 tbsp. teriyaki sauce (page 36)

black sesame seeds
cilantro leaves

Prepare the octopus as described on page 74. As the best use for the thick parts of the tentacles is in nigiri sushi, it is okay to use the smaller ends of the tentacles in this recipe.

Place the julienned cucumber on a plate, arrange the octopus on top, and spoon over it a teaspoon of teriyaki sauce. Sprinkle sesame seeds and cilantro leaves. (Or you can make little fans with the cucumber as shown in the picture, adding a more decorative touch.)

Makes 1 portion

ankimo monkfish liver

see variations page 218

There are plenty of things that come out of our sea that we in the West tend to discard, and monkfish liver is just one example. In Japan they are described as the "foie gras of the sea," and indeed, they are not dissimilar.

1 monkfish liver
1 qt. water
1 oz. salt

1 tsp. ceviche sauce (page 43)
1 tsp. caviar

As always, make sure that your fishmonger is certain that the monkfish liver is fresh. Remove blood vessels and the membrane from the outside with a small knife. Soak the liver in salted water for about 30 minutes. You may need more than the one quart if the liver is large.

Pat dry. Put the liver on a piece of plastic wrap and roll it into a cylindrical shape. Pierce a few holes in the plastic wrap. Next, wrap the liver in aluminum foil. Tighten the liver-sausage shape at both ends, then wrap it in a bamboo maki rolling mat and secure with a rubber band. Steam in a colander over boiling water for 45 minutes.

Pour the ceviche sauce onto a plate. Once cool, cut the sausage-shaped liver into 1-in. thick slices and arrange on top of the sauce. Spoon a teaspoon of caviar on top.

Makes 1 portion

korean-style sashimi & korean chili sauce

see variations page 219

Korea is another country that enjoys serving fish in its raw state, but consistent with traditional Korean cuisine, they tend to add more flavor in the form of punchy chile and garlic. In addition, they add plenty of vegetables, which are often lacking on restaurant menus in Japan, although at home the Japanese eat a wide variety of vegetables.

1 oz. salmon fillet
1 oz. tuna fillet
1 oz. whitefish, such as sea bass fillet
2 oz. shari rice (page 28)
2 tsp. red cabbage, finely sliced

2 tsp. tsuma daikon white radish
1/2 tsp. micro greens
shiso cress
4 tsp. Korean chili sauce (page 54)

Chop each of the fish fillets into small cubes. Place a ball of shari rice in the center of the bowl and arrange the red cabbage slices, shredded white radish, and micro greens around it in a circular pattern. Place the three kinds of fish between the vegetables.

Decorate with micro greens and shiso cress. Serve the Korean chili dressing in a pouring vessel so that it can be added to the dish as desired.

Makes 1 portion

variations

tamago sweet omelet sashimi

see base recipe page 189

tamago with brown shrimp
Prepare the basic recipe, adding 1 3/4 oz. small, raw brown shrimps to the egg mixture before cooking.

tamago with shiitake mushroom
Prepare the basic recipe, adding 1 3/4 oz. shiitake mushrooms, rehydrated in dashi and soy and chopped, to the egg mixture before cooking.

tamago, mitsuba & halloumi
Prepare the basic recipe, adding chopped halloumi cheese and mitsuba leaf or chives to the egg mixture before cooking.

tamago & green pepper
Prepare the basic recipe, adding chopped raw green pepper to egg mixture before cooking.

tamago with ham
Prepare the basic recipe, adding small pieces of chopped ham to the egg mixture before cooking.

tamago & chestnut
Prepare the basic recipe, adding chopped re-boiled chestnuts to egg mixture before cooking.

variations

whitefish sashimi of red mullet, leeks & ginger oroshi

see base recipe page 190

lemon sole, ginger oroshi & leeks
Prepare the basic recipe, replacing mullet with sole. You might want to fillet gomai 5 fillets rather than sanmai 3 fillets as described on page 18, if it is a large sole.

john dory, ikura salmon roe & chives
Prepare the basic recipe, replacing mullet with John Dory. Replace leeks and ginger oroshi with salmon roe and chopped chives.

red snapper & ume plum
Prepare the basic recipe, replacing mullet with red snapper. Serve on a bed of tsuma, shredded cucumber, and daikon, and a dab of ume plum on each slice of snapper. Omit leeks and ginger oroshi.

dover sole & caviar
Prepare the basic recipe, replacing mullet with dover sole. You might want to fillet gomai 5 fillets rather than sanmai 3 fillets as described on page 18, if it is a large sole. Decorate with caviar.

variations

hamachi yellowtail sashimi, herb ceviche sauce & ponzu olive oil

see base recipe page 193

salmon sashimi herb ceviche, daikon & ponzu olive oil
Prepare the basic recipe, replacing yellowtail with salmon slices.

tuna sashimi herb ceviche, shallot & ponzu olive oil
Prepare the basic recipe, replacing the yellowtail with tuna, and center daikon tsuma with thinly sliced shallot.

scallop sashimi, jalapeño salsa, daikon & lime olive oil
Prepare the basic recipe, replacing yellowtail with raw scallop sashimi slices, omitting the ponzu. Drizzle the scallop with a little lime juice and olive oil. Replace the herb ceviche with jalapeño salsa (page 54).

ama ebi sweet shrimp sashimi, jalapeño salsa, daikon & lime olive oil
Prepare the basic recipe, replacing yellowtail with raw ama ebi, omitting the ponzu. Drizzle the shrimp with a little lime juice and olive oil. Replace the ceviche with jalapeño salsa (page 54).

marinated sashimi of mackerel, scallion & oroshi ginger

see base recipe page 194

vinegared sardine sashimi

Prepare the basic recipe, replacing mackerel with sardines and shortening the marinating time by 45 minutes. Take time to cut the diagonal slices in the sardine flesh to reveal the contrasting redder flesh below. Top with chopped scallion.

vinegared herring sashimi

Prepare the basic recipe, replacing mackerel with herring. Top with chives and shiso cress.

aji no tataki horse mackerel sashimi

Prepare the horse mackerel as described on page 94 and mix with ponzu sauce and chopped scallion.

tororo mountain yam potato & marinated tuna sashmi

Prepare the basic recipe, replacing tsuma with julienned slices of a large, 6-in. chunk of Japanese mountain yam potato, or nagaimo. Add 1 3/4 oz. tuna, cubed and marinated with sweet soy marinade (page 222) rather than the vinegar and serve with chopped scallion.

variations

usuzukuri thinly sliced turbot, ponzu, oroshi daikon & shiso cress

see base recipe page 196

lemon sole usuzukuri sashimi
Prepare the basic recipe, replacing turbot with lemon sole.

wrasse usuzukuri sashimi
Prepare the basic recipe, replacing turbot with wrasse prepared in the 3-fillet method described on pages 16–17.

seared beef usuzukuri sashimi, nashi pear & tamari sesame oil dressing
Marinate 4–5 oz. marbled sirloin or rib-eye beef in a mixture of soy, mirin, and rice vinegar for at least an hour. Place in a colander and pour boiling water over the beef to sear the outside. Cut into very thin slices. Cut a whole medium-size and very ripe nashi pear into thin julienned strips. Arrange the beef slices on a plate, cover with the julienned pear, and drizzle with a mixture of tamari and sesame oil. Sprinkle with sesame seeds.

megrim & shiso cress usuzukuri sashimi
Prepare the basic recipe, replacing turbot with megrim and decorating with purple shiso cress in the ponzu sauce.

seared duck usuzukuri sashimi, nashi pear & tamari sesame oil dressing
Follow the seared beef usuzukuri recipe above, replacing beef with a duck breast.

aburi salmon sashimi ceviche & truffle olive oil

see base recipe page 198

ebi tiger shrimp sashimi, ceviche & truffle olive oil
Prepare the basic recipe, replacing salmon with 8–10 whole, large raw shrimp. Aburi
blowtorch the shrimp and cut into 3/4-in. pieces. Decorate with micro greens and a little
lime juice in your truffle olive oil.

scallop sashimi ceviche & truffle olive oil
Prepare the basic recipe, replacing salmon with 3–4 whole, large, dive-caught scallops. Aburi
blowtorch the scallops and cut into 3/4-in. pieces. Decorate as above.

white tuna sashimi ceviche, hijki & truffle olive oil
Prepare the basic recipe, replacing salmon with albacore tuna slices and decorate with
rehydrated hijiki seaweed and truffle olive oil.

lobster sashimi ceviche, cilantro & truffle olive oil
Prepare the basic recipe, replacing salmon with 5 oz. raw lobster meat. Aburi blowtorch the
lobster meat, spoon the ceviche dressing over it. Finish by sprinkling with cilantro leaves, and
drizzling small drops of truffle oil over all.

monkfish sashimi ceviche, cilantro & truffle olive oil
Prepare the basic recipe, replacing salmon with 5 oz. raw monkfish tail. Aburi blowtorch the
monkfish tail, spoon the ceviche dressing over it. Finish as above.

variations

sesame-encrusted salmon sashimi
& spicy korean chili dressing

see base recipe page 201

sesame-encrusted cod sashimi & jalapeño salsa

Prepare the basic recipe, replacing salmon with cod and the Korean chili sauce with jalapeño salsa (page 54).

sesame-encrusted tofu & jalapeño salsa sashimi

Prepare the basic recipe, replacing salmon with 5 oz. (about half of a standard pack size) firm tofu.

salt-and-pepper-encrusted salmon sashimi & apple–mustard sauce

Coat the salmon fillet with crushed black pepper and sea salt. Serve on the apple–mustard sauce (page 54).

salt-and-pepper-encrusted yellowtail sashimi & apple–mustard sauce

Prepare the basic recipe, replacing salmon with yellowtail fillet. Coat the yellowtail fillet with crushed black pepper and sea salt, and serve on the apple–mustard sauce (page 54).

salt-and-pink-pepper-encrusted beef sashimi, shallot & apple–mustard sauce

Prepare the basic recipe, replacing salmon with 5 oz. beef fillet. Coat the fillet with crushed pink pepper and sea salt, thinly slice the shallot and put in the center. Serve on the apple–mustard sauce (page 54).

squid sashimi & ikura salmon roe

see base recipe page 202

squid sashimi & mentaiko spicy pollock roe
Prepare the basic recipe, adding 2 teaspoons of pollock roe to the squid.

oyster, shallots & ponzu
Prepare the basic recipe, replacing squid with a large, shucked oyster. Add a teaspoon of ponzu sauce (page 39) and finely chopped shallot to the shell.

octopus ceviche & cilantro
Prepare the basic recipe, replacing squid with raw octopus. Cut into slices rather than julienne strips and serve with ceviche sauce (page 43) and cilantro leaves.

cuttlefish sashimi, ink & ikura salmon roe
Prepare the basic recipe, replacing squid with cuttlefish. Marinate the salmon roe with the ink of the cuttlefish, soy sauce, and sake.

octopus sashimi, teriyaki & sesame

see base recipe page 205

cuttlefish sashimi & teriyaki
Prepare the basic recipe, replacing octopus with lightly boiled or
steamed cuttlefish.

shrimp sashimi, soy sauce & sesame
Prepare the basic recipe, replacing octopus with shrimp cooked as described on
page 225. Heat a mixture of soy sauce, mirin, and sake. When cool, spoon it over
the shrimp and sprinkle with sesame seeds. Place on top of julienned cucumber.

jellyfish sashimi, soy sauce & sesame
Prepare the basic recipe, replacing octopus with jellyfish. Normally you will
find them dried and sliced in an Asian grocery. They need to be soaked overnight
and then soaked again for 30 minutes in fresh water. Roll up the flesh and
slice it into thin julienne strips. Blanch the strips in boiling water then immerse
them in ice water. Heat a mixture of soy sauce, mirin, and sake. When cool, mix
with a tablespoon of toasted sesame oil, and spoon it over the jellyfish and
sprinkle with sesame seeds. Place on top of the julienned cucumber.

variations

ankimo monkfish liver

see base recipe page 206

shirako cod milt
You will probably need to ask your fishmonger to obtain this for you. The sperm sack is best served in a small bowl, topped with chopped scallions, wasabi, and ponzu sauce (page 39).

ikura salmon roe
Marinate the salmon roe in a mixture of soy and sake for at least 4 hours. Pour off the liquid, taking care not to break the eggs. Serve with soy and wasabi in a hollowed-out piece of cucumber.

uni sea urchin
Serve the urchins just as they are in a piece of hollowed-out cucumber, with soy and wasabi.

kazunoko herring roe
Herring roe has a fantastic crunchy texture. Serve on a bed of wakame seaweed with soy and wasabi.

variations

korean-style sashimi & korean chili sauce

see base recipe page 208

scallops, cockles, spinach & korean sashimi
Replace fish with 2 large scallops and 1 oz. cockles (out of shell weight). Both the cockles and scallops can be served raw, but you can also steam them if you prefer. Serve with wilted spinach tossed in a little sesame oil instead of the micro greens.

tofu & spinach korean sashimi
Marinate a block of tofu in soy, mirin, and rice vinegar. Cut into 3/4-in. cubes and arrange over the rice, with wilted spinach tossed in sesame oil, julienned carrot, and julienned cucumber.

raw beef, pear & quail egg korean sashimi
This dish is inspired by Korea's famous dish of raw beef and pear. Chop 1 3/4 oz. marbled sirloin or rib-eye beef coarsely. Arrange julienned cucumber, julienned carrot, and julienned pear over the rice. Top with the beef and decorate with a raw quail egg.

temaki hand roll

Temaki really do have to be made just before you want to eat them, because if you leave the nori wrapped around the rice for even a few minutes, the crispness is lost and you are left having to tear into the temaki with all the pleasurable textures gone. Thus they are not ideal for picnics or parties, unless you want to get your friends around a table making their own.

yellowfin tuna, scallion & wasabi mayonnaise temaki hand roll

see variations page 237

Temaki are usually served right at the end of a sushi dinner, when you are replete with sashimi and nigiri. The recipe here and its variations require super-fresh slices of raw fish, but unlike sashimi and nigiri cuts, they can be sliced from the shorter ends of the fish, so nothing is wasted. Temaki is mostly about getting the rolling technique right. After that, you can fill them with any number of things.

1/2 oz. yellowfin tuna fillet
1/2 sheet nori
1 oz. shari rice (page 28)
wasabi

2 tsp. diagonally cut scallion
white sesame seeds
1 tsp. wasabi mayonnaise (page 50)

Cut the tuna into 2-in. long slices. To make the temaki shape, be sure your left hand is dry and place the nori horizontally across your palm, holding it between your thumb and four fingers. Dip your right hand in vinegar water and pick up the rice. Spread it on the left-side of the nori. Dab a little wasabi paste over the rice to your liking. Once your rice is on the nori, dry your right hand and arrange the tuna slices and scallion on the rice. Sprinkle with sesame seeds. Clean and dry your right hand again. The nori is now flat on your left palm. Pick up the bottom left corner of the nori with your right hand and pull it over the filling, aiming for the top of the nori sheet, and deftly tuck it under the filling. Gently turn with the left thumb to make an ice-cream-cone shape. Spoon a little wasabi mayonnaise over it to taste.

Makes 1 temaki

unagi faux eel kabayaki
& cucumber temaki hand roll

see variations page 238

The sweet soy-basted faux eel is a particular favorite. It is well placed toward the end of a dinner when its denser texture and stronger tastes won't subvert the more delicate morsels — whitefish nigiri for example.

1 fillet of a dense whitefish (We use lesser
    spotted dogfish, a kind of shark.)
1 cup soy sauce
1/3 cup sugar
1/3 cup mirin

1/3 cup sake
1/2 oz. cucumber, cut into thick, 2-in. lengths
1/2 sheet nori
1 oz. shari rice (page 28)
white sesame seeds

Eel populations are in serious danger of collapse. There are only two spawning grounds in the world, and both are dangerously overfished. Because eels can live until they are 80 and mate only once in their lives — just before they die — it is easy to see why they have become so vulnerable to overfishing. The wonder of this dish is that by cooking a good dense fish the same way as unagi is prepared in Japan, you get a really close alternative.

We use the lesser spotted dogfish, which is both abundant and virtually unused in the West. Get your fishmonger to fillet it and remove the skin, as it is tough and will dull your knife.

Wash under cold water. Combine the soy, sugar, mirin, and sake until the sugar is dissolved. Place the fillet in half of the marinade (reserve the remaining half) and leave overnight in the refrigerator. Remove the fillet from the marinade and place it in a steamer for 10 minutes. Then put under a broiler, basting a little more of the reserved marinade sauce on top, and broil until the surface is crisp. Reduce the remaining liquid and, when thickened, set aside to reserve for basting over the faux eel. Cut the broiled fillet into 2-in. slices. Shape the temaki as described in the first recipe, page 221, and sprinkle with sesame seeds to serve.

Makes 1 temaki, though there is enough fish fillet to make many more

ebi tiger shrimp, avocado & wasabi mayonnaise temaki

see variations page 239

Cooked shellfish make excellent crunchy fillings in a temaki.

1 raw tiger shrimp
1 qt. water
salt
1/2 cup mirin
1/2 cup rice vinegar

1/2 sheet nori
1 oz. shari rice (page 28)
1 tbsp. avocado, cut into thick 2-in. lengths
white sesame seeds
1 tsp. wasabi mayonnaise

You only use one shrimp in each temaki but make as many hand rolls as you like. Skewer a whole, raw shrimp from the tail to head just under the top shell. Drop the shrimp into a pan of boiling, salted water and cook until the color changes from translucent gray to pink, about 3 minutes. Remove from the water and cool, then remove the skewers. The shrimp is cooked when it is bouncy to the touch. Pull off the head and peel the shrimp carefully. Taking care to leave the tail intact, remove the shell and legs. Pat dry. Make an incision with a small sharp knife at the top of the inside of the shrimp. Gently cut down to the tail so as to butterfly-open the shrimp, taking care not to cut through the flesh. Wash under running water to remove any gray innards clinging under the spine.

Combine the mirin and vinegar and marinate the shrimp for 30 minutes in the refrigerator. Remove and pat dry. After that you can use immediately, or easily store them in the freezer. Roll the temaki as described on page 221, including the avocado slices, and sprinkle with sesame seeds. Spoon a little wasabi mayonnaise over it to taste.
Makes 1 temaki

crisp salmon skin teriyaki
& scallion temaki hand roll

see variations page 240

Teriyaki flavors are good to finish a sushi dinner with. Robust in flavor, they should come after the more delicate raw fish in sashimi and nigiri.

3/4 oz. of salmon skin (try to leave a thin layer of salmon flesh under the skin)
salt
1 tsp. teriyaki sauce (page 36)

1/2 sheet nori
1 oz. shari rice (page 28)
2 tsp. finely chopped scallion

Take the salmon skin pieces, cover lightly with sea salt on both sides, and place under a broiler until it is crispy brown and the skin starts to bubble and darken. Set aside to cool. It should now feel nearly brittle.

Cut the salmon skin into long lengths and brush with the teriyaki sauce. Make the temaki with the scallion as described on page 221.

Makes 1 temaki

negitoro tuna, mayonnaise & scallion temaki hand roll

see variations page 241

The taste of toro tuna was probably what first led me to open a sushi bar; the creaminess of the flesh of the belly of the bluefin tuna is quite divine. Bluefin tuna fetch extraordinary prices these days, the record recently being about $730,000 for one fish! The astonishing decline of bluefin stocks has been well documented. I simply can't bring myself to profit at the expense of such a beautiful and noble creature, so toro came off our menus in 1998. And I can honestly say that I've not missed it — now I much prefer to see these incredible animals on television as they circumnavigate the globe with their intelligence and awesome grace.

3/4 oz. yellowfin tuna fillet, the end of the cut is fine
1 tsp. wasabi mayonnaise (page 50)

1/2 sheet nori
1 oz. shari rice (page 28)
2 tsp. finely chopped scallion

Makes one temaki, but make up as much of the tuna mix as you like.

Mince your tuna very finely, using a large knife and chopping it until it becomes soft and mushy. Mix with the wasabi mayonnaise.

Make the temaki with the scallion as described on page 221.

Makes 1 temaki

natto fermented soybean
& scallion temaki hand roll

see variations page 242

This section features a selection of classic Japanese vegetarian ingredients, which are often some of the hardest for non-Japanese people to get their head around. Natto fermented soybean has become a personal favorite of mine, but it took me a long time, and a flight on a Japanese airline with little to eat but dried natto snacks, to finally acquire the taste. Once someone in Japan realizes that you are quite familiar with their culture, their next question is always "So, can you eat natto?" Not to be outdone in the culinary stakes, I persevered, and now I love the stuff.

1 tbsp. natto fermented soybean	1 oz. shari rice (page 28)
1/2 sheet nori	2 tsp. finely chopped scallion

Fermenting soybeans to become natto is a step too far for the scope of this book, and natto is commonly purchased in tubes or small plastic packets that can be frozen. It doesn't last long once opened, so the frozen option is a good one.

Make the temaki with the natto and scallion as described on page 221. Use a teaspoon or chopsticks to spread the natto because you will soon appreciate its peculiar gooey and sticky traits!

Makes 1 temaki

pumpkin & burdock tempura temaki hand roll

see variations page 243

Tempura, long associated with Japan, was probably a legacy of the sixteenth-century Portuguese missionaries who would eat only fish on Fridays and often deep-fried it. The word itself is thought to be a Japanification of templo, the Portuguese word for temple. Nontraditional in Japan, tempura sushi rolls are a solid favorite in the West.

1 burdock root
1/2 pumpkin, cut into medium juliennes about 2-in. long
1 tsp rice vinegar

batter for 4 rolls
1 cup all-purpose flour, plus a little extra for coating

1 large egg
1 1/2 cups ice water and ice cubes

vegetable oil, for deep-frying
2 nori sheets
5 oz. shari rice (page 28)
white sesame seeds
chili mayonnaise (page 50)

Burdock comes in a long muddy root. Scrub (rather than peel) the outside well to remove the dirt. Lightly scrape off the skin with a knife (burdock is deemed to be a very healthy root, and much of the nutrient and flavor content lies just under the skin, so best preserve it). Cut into medium julienned strips about 2-in. long; do the same for the pumpkin. Once cut, place them in a bowl of cold water with a teaspoon of rice vinegar in it to avoid discoloring.

Now make the tempura batter. The secret is not to beat the batter too vigorously, so mix the flour, egg, and ice water with chopsticks and leave lumps of flour unblended. You can also add ice cubes if you like.

Heat the vegetable oil in a small deep pan to 350°F. Alternatively, you can test the temperature by flicking in a drop of batter: It should sink and then rise; if it just sinks it is too cool, and if it rises straight away it is too hot. Coat the burdock and pumpkin juliennes in a little flour, remove the excess flour, then dip into the batter. Immerse in the hot oil for about 3 minutes, or until the batter has turned golden. Remove the vegetables with a stainless mesh spoon and drain on a wire rack or paper towels.

Make the temaki with the tempura vegetables as described on page 221. Sprinkle with sesame seeds and serve with chili mayonnaise.

Makes 4 temaki

katsu chicken, cucumber & tonkatsu mayonnaise temaki hand roll

see variations page 244

Breaded and deep-fried dishes make popular lunchtime meals, and tonkatsu, breaded and deep-fried pork, is nearly always served along with shredded white cabbage and tonkatsu sauce, a spicy (but not hot) thick brown sauce. In the West we use chicken, which feels better suited to sushi, though neither would be found in traditional sushi.

vegetable oil, for frying
1 egg
3 1/2 oz. fillet chicken breast or thigh
salt and pepper to season
2 tbsp. all-purpose flour
5 tbsp. breadcrumbs

2 nori sheets
5 oz. shari rice (page 28)
2 oz. julienned cucumber
tonkatsu mayonnaise (page 50)
shiso cress, to garnish

Heat the oil in a deep pan to 350°F degrees. Beat the egg. Sprinkle the chicken with salt and pepper. Line up the beaten egg, a plate of flour, and a plate of breadcrumbs side by side. Coat the chicken with the flour, shake off the excess, then dip in the beaten egg, then into the breadcrumbs and straight into the hot oil. Cook until crisp and golden brown on the outside, remove with a long slotted spoon and drain on paper towels. Cut the chicken into four diagonal slices. Make the temaki with a slice of katsu chicken and cucumber as described in the recipe on page 221, spooning some tonkatsu mayonnaise and a sprinkle of shiso cress over it.
Makes 4 temaki

tuna salad with corn temaki

see variations page 245

Sushi tends to favor raw fish, but there are a few things that work well cooked in temaki, and canned tuna is easy and versatile to use, and a relatively common stuffing in everyday, homemade sushi.

5 oz. canned tuna in water
4 tsp. finely chopped onion
1 oz. corn

6 tsp. wasabi mayonnaise (page 50)
3 sheets nori
7 1/2 oz. shari rice (page 28)

Drain the canned tuna. Combine the tuna, onion, corn, and wasabi mayonnaise together. Make the temaki as described in the recipe on page 221.

Makes 6 temaki

variations

yellowfin tuna, scallion & wasabi mayonnaise temaki hand roll

see base recipe page 221

salmon & avocado temaki
Prepare the basic recipe, replacing tuna with salmon and avocado slices, a sprinkle of sesame seed, and wasabi mayonnaise.

bream, shiso cress, cucumber & yuzukosho temaki
Prepare the basic recipe, replacing tuna with slices of bream and cucumber, shiso cress and a dab of yuzukosho paste.

sea bass, red radish, cucumber & jalapeño salsa temaki
Prepare the basic recipe, replacing tuna with slices of sea bass and cucumber, finely sliced red radish, and a teaspoon of jalapeño salsa (page 54).

hamachi yellowtail, scallion & tobiko flying fish roe temaki
Prepare the basic recipe, adding a teaspoon of flying fish roe.

mackerel, asparagus, shiso cress & yuzu mayonnaise temaki
Prepare the basic recipe, replacing tuna with slices of mackerel, blanched asparagus, 1 teaspoon mustard, and shiso cress and a teaspoon of yuzu mayonnaise (page 34).

hamachi yellowtail, red radish, red pepper & jalapeño salsa temaki
Prepare the basic recipe, adding red radish, red pepper, and jalapeño salsa (page 54).

variations

unagi faux eel kabayaki & cucumber temaki hand roll

see base recipe page 222

duck leg, cucumber, chile & chives temaki
Prepare the basic recipe, replacing faux eel with meat from a duck leg. Roll with finely chopped chile and chives.

beef fillet, red onion & mizuna temaki
Prepare the basic recipe, replacing faux eel with 1/2 oz. marbled sirloin or rib-eye beef, omitting the steaming stage. Thinly slice the red onions and roll with mizuna.

enoki mushrooms & mizuna temaki
Prepare the basic recipe, replacing faux eel with enoki mushrooms, which don't need marinating and won't take long under the broiler. Roll with mizuna leaves and a sprinkle of sesame seeds.

unagi faux eel kabayaki dogfish, green beans & avocado temaki
Prepare the basic recipe, adding blanched green beans and a slice of avocado.

variations

ebi tiger shrimp, avocado & wasabi mayonnaise temaki

see base recipe page 225

shrimp, mizuna, pine nuts & yuzu mayonnaise temaki
Prepare the basic recipe. Roll with mizuna leaves, yuzu mayonnaise, and pine nuts.

shrimp, ikura salmon roe & lettuce temaki
Prepare the basic recipe, and roll with lettuce leaves. Top with salmon roe.

squid, cucumber & ume plum temaki
Prepare the basic recipe, replacing shrimp with julienned strips of raw squid as prepared on page 17. Add julienne slices of cucumber and a dash of ume plum paste.

crab & avocado temaki
Prepare the basic recipe, replacing shrimp with 1/2 oz. mixed fresh brown and white crabmeat. Add some slices of avocado, and sprinkle with sesame seeds.

crab, scallion & yuzu mayonnaise temaki
Prepare the basic recipe, replacing shrimp with 3/4 oz. mixed fresh brown and white crabmeat. Add some chopped scallion and a teaspoon of yuzu mayonnaise (page 34).

lobster, avocado, tobiko flying fish roe & wasabi mayonnaise temaki
Prepare the basic recipe, replacing shrimp with lobster as prepared on page 62. Add slices of avocado, flying fish roe, and wasabi mayonnaise (page 50).

crisp salmon skin teriyaki & scallion temaki hand roll

see base recipe page 226

chicken skin teriyaki, cucumber & mizuna temaki
Prepare the basic recipe, replacing salmon skin with chicken skin. Wrap the temaki, using slices of cucumber and mizuna leaves.

beef teriyaki, green beans & watercress temaki
Crisp a few slices of beef under a broiler, basting with teriyaki sauce. Blanch the green beans and wrap them with sprigs of watercress.

squid teriyaki & asparagus temaki
Broil a few slices of squid, basting with teriyaki sauce. Wrap with blanched asparagus.

teriyaki quail, fig & lettuce temaki
Broil a few slices of quail meat, basting with teriyaki sauce. Wrap with fig slices and lettuce.

teriyaki shiitake mushroom, burdock & sesame temaki
Rehydrate the shiitake by soaking in water for 20 minutes. Prepare and cool burdock and mushrooms as described on page 252. Spoon over a little teriyaki sauce.

shishito pepper & red pepper teriyaki temaki
Halve and deseed 1 whole shishito and cut two 2-in. lengths of red pepper. Broil, basting with teriyaki sauce. Cut to size and wrap. Sprinkle with shiso cress or mustard and cress.

negitoro tuna, mayonnaise & scallion temaki hand roll

see base recipe page 228

chopped salmon & cucumber temaki
Prepare the basic recipe, replacing tuna with salmon, and wrap the temaki with julienned cucumber. Squeeze over a little lime juice to serve.

chopped scallop & shiso leaf temaki
Prepare the basic recipe, replacing tuna with 1/2 a whole, large scallop, chopped. Mix with some shredded shiso leaf and minced shallots. Combine this with yuzu mayonnaise and add a dash of lime juice.

chopped snapper in ceviche dressing, mizuna & shiso cress temaki
Prepare the basic recipe, replacing tuna with chopped snapper (any firm bream or flatfish will do). Mix with a teaspoon of ceviche sauce (page 43). Wrap the temaki with the ceviche snapper, adding mizuna and shiso cress.

chopped yellowtail & scallion temaki
Prepare the basic recipe, replacing tuna with yellowtail ("hamachi" or "buri" in Japanese).

chopped sea bass & shiso leaf temaki
Prepare the basic recipe, replacing tuna with sea bass. Mix with some shredded shiso leaf and minced shallots. Combine this with yuzu mayonnaise and add a dash of lime juice.

variations

natto fermented soybean & scallion temaki hand roll

see base recipe page 230

umeboshi pickled plum & cucumber temaki
Replace natto with umeboshi. Umeboshi can be found in Japanese groceries, or in health food shops, with the best quality brand in Europe being Clearspring. To make the wrap, use the paste form, or mash the whole plum yourself, adding plenty of cucumber to cool down the tartness.

natto fermented soybean & okra temaki
Prepare the basic recipe, adding a sprinkling of chopped okra.

umeboshi pickled plum, daikon radish & green bean temaki
Make a temaki using blanched green beans, julienned strips of daikon radish, and a dab of ume plum.

umeboshi pickled plum & shiso temaki
Shred some shiso leaves, add julienned cucumber, and dab on some ume plum. Ume and shiso are a classic combination.

simmered bamboo & cucumber temaki
Prepare bamboo as described on page 247. Make the wrap with julienned cucumber and sprinkle with sesame seeds.

variations

pumpkin & burdock tempura temaki hand roll

see base recipe page 232

tempura softshell crab, avocado & chili mayonnaise temaki
Prepare the basic recipe, replacing burdock with softshell crab cut into quarters.
Wrap using a teaspoon of chili mayonnaise (page 50) and slices of avocado.
Scatter flying fish roe over the temaki.

tempura shrimp, cos lettuce, avocado & wasabi mayonnaise temaki
Prepare the basic recipe, replacing burdock with shrimp, leaving the tails on for
a decorative effect. Wrap using a teaspoon of wasabi mayonnaise (page 50),
slices of avocado, and lettuce leaves. Scatter with torn shiso cress.

tempura squid, mizuna, chile, sea salt & lime temaki
Prepare the basic recipe, replacing burdock with squid. Wrap with mizuna leaves,
chopped red chile, and sprinkle with a little sea salt and lime zest.

tempura avocado & smoked paprika mayonnaise temaki
Prepare the basic recipe, replacing burdock with 1 quartered avocado. Wrap
using a teaspoon of smoked paprika mayonnaise (page 50).

tempura zucchini flower stuffed with burrata temaki
Stuff a zucchini flower with burrata cheese and carefully seal the flower before
coating it in batter and frying. Wrap, spooning on a teaspoon of honey to taste.

variations

katsu chicken, cucumber & tonkatsu mayonnaise temaki hand roll

see base recipe page 234

tonkatsu pork & white cabbage temaki
Prepare the basic recipe, replacing chicken with fried fillet of pork. Wrap with shredded white cabbage and a spoonful of tonkatsu mayonnaise.

shrimp katsu, mizuna & wasabi mayonnaise temaki
Prepare the basic recipe, replacing chicken with four tiger shrimp in fried breadcrumbs, katsu style, and wrap with mizuna leaves and wasabi mayonnaise (page 50).

shrimp katsu, avocado & chili mayonnaise temaki
Prepare the basic recipe, replacing chicken with shrimp in fried breadcrumbs, katsu style, and wrap with a slice of avocado and sweet chili mayonnaise (page 50).

shirako cod milt katsu, lettuce heart & jalapeño salsa temaki
Prepare the basic recipe, replacing chicken with shrimp in fried breadcrumbs, katsu style, and 3 oz. shirako, the sperm sac of cod from a Japanese supermarket. Wrap the shirako katsu with contrasting crunchy lettuce hearts, and a spoonful of jalapeño salsa (page 54).

salmon katsu, avocado, scallion & yuzu mayonnaise temaki
Prepare the basic recipe, replacing chicken with salmon in fried breadcrumbs, katsu style, and wrap with a slice of avocado. Add chopped scallion and a spoonful of yuzu mayonnaise.

tuna salad with corn temaki

see base recipe page 236

tuna salad with red radish, watercress & onion temaki
Prepare the basic recipe, adding onion, red radish and wasabi mayonnaise.

kakuni poached salmon, watercress & wasabi mayonnaise temaki
Prepare the basic recipe, replacing tuna with salmon poached as described on page 256.
Mix with the mayonnaise and wrap with watercress.

kakuni poached salmon, arugula & wasabi mayonnaise temaki
Prepare the basic recipe, replacing tuna with salmon poached as described on page 256.
Mix with the wasabi mayonnaise and wrap with arugula leaves.

kakuni tuna, soy & ginger temaki
Prepare the basic recipe, replacing canned tuna with tuna poached as described on page 256.
Mix with the wasabi mayonnaise and wrap with arugula leaves and oroshi ginger.

kakuni sea bass, cucumber & katsuo boshi bonito temaki
Prepare the basic recipe, replacing tuna with sea bass poached as described on page 256.
Mix with wasabi mayonnaise and a sprinkle of katsuo boshi. Wrap with julienned cucumber.

chirashi, onigiri & pressed sushi

While sushi is generally considered the purview of experts, chirashi, inari, and onigiri are all types of sushi that are commonly made at home. They generally require less knife technique, and rice molding skills are less needed. Their versatility means that you can often use whatever leftover fish or vegetables you may have on hand.

chirashi of shiitake mushroom, lotus root & bamboo

see variations page 269

Chirashi means "scattered sushi," and usually refers to raw fish. Here though we use vegetables.

3 shiitake mushrooms

marinade
1/2 cup soy sauce
3 tbsp. sake
3 tbsp. apple juice or 3 tbsp. sugar

1/2 renkon lotus root, cut into very thin slices and then into quarters, reserving 2 whole slices for decoration

1/2 takenoko bamboo shoot (from a can or vacuum pack), cut into 2-in. lengths
1 carrot, cut into 3/4-in. diagonal chunks
5 runner beans cut into diagonal 1 1/2-in. lengths, or green beans
1/4 pouch of abura-age fried tofu
4 tsp. tamago omelet (page 189, not strictly necessary but very traditional)
1/4 nori sheet, shredded
7 oz. shari rice (page 28) or genmai brown rice

Place the shiitake in 1 cup of hot water and leave to rehydrate for about 20 minutes. Remove the shiitake and combine 1 cup of hot water with the soy, sake, and apple juice in a small saucepan. Put the shiitake, lotus root, bamboo, and carrot into the saucepan and bring to a boil. Simmer for about 4 minutes, until the liquid has nearly evaporated. Steam or blanch the runner beans, plunge into cold water, and add to the cooled other vegetables. Cut the abura-age into 3/4-in. long, fine strips. Finely shred the tamago sweet omlete and the nori seaweed. Place the warm rice in a bowl. Arrange the vegetables on top, scatter the green beans, abuara-age, and omelet on top, and decorate with the lotus root and shredded nori.

Makes 1 bowl

classic chirashi scattered fish

see variations page 270

This is the classic Tokyo-style scattered fish on a bowl of rice. There are no set rules as to which fish to choose here, so pick your favorites.

1 tsp. dried wakame seaweed
7 oz. shari rice (page 28)
4 tsp. shredded daikon
1 shiso leaf
3 slices of salmon, cut as sashimi
3 slices of snapper or bream, cut as sashimi
3 slices of marinated mackerel, cut as sashimi
3 slices of tuna
2 boiled tiger shrimp

2 slices of boiled octopus
2 large strips of tamago omelet (page 189)
lemon slices
1 tsp. ikura salmon roe
wasabi
1 tsp. pickled ginger
julienned cucumber
1 tsp. shiso cress or mustard and cress

Rehydrate the wakame seaweed in a little water for a few minutes, drain well. Fill a bowl with sushi rice. Classic white rice works best, but you can use genmai brown rice if you prefer. Arrange the grated daikon at the far edge of the bowl alongside the wakame. Place the shiso leaf on top of the daikon.

Arrange the slices of fish and omelet as you like over the rice, taking into consideration the balance of color. Add slices of lemon alongside the whitefish (snapper or bream) to add contrast. Decorate with ikura salmon roe.

Place a dab of wasabi to one side. Garnish with a piece of pickled ginger, julienned cucumber, and shiso cress.

Makes 1 bowl

seared beef chirashi with red wine & wasabi jus

see variations page 271

This is a totally unconventional chirashi, and I feel traditionalists around the world recoiling in horror! Too delicious not to include here, it proves that it's worth trying something new.

4 tsp. daikon oroshi grated white radish
1/2 chile
1/4 red onion
ice water
3 tbsp. wasabi powder
2 tbsp. water
4 tbsp. soy sauce
3 tbsp. mirin

4 oz. beef fillet
sea salt and pepper
2 tsp. butter for frying
3 tbsp. red wine
white truffle oil
1 tsp. sansho peppercorns (or pink peppercorns)
7 oz. shari rice (page 28)
2 tsp. scallion, finely chopped

Mix the grated daikon with finely chopped chile. Finely slice the red onion and place in a bowl of ice water for 10 minutes. Drain and set aside. Mix the wasabi powder with the water until dissolved, and blend with the soy sauce. Add the mirin to the soy–wasabi liquid. Rub salt and pepper into the beef fillet. Heat butter in a pan and sear the fillet, about 1 minute on each side. Keeping the beef juices in the pan, add the soy, wasabi, and mirin mix and use a high heat to reduce. Add the red wine and reduce further. Last, add a splash of white truffle oil and sansho peppercorns. Slice the beef fillet to make a sashimi-style appearance. Fill a bowl two-thirds full with shari rice and arrange the beef slices on top. Pour on a little of the red wine wasabi jus and garnish with the sliced red onion, scallion, and chili oroshi daikon. Serve the remainder of the red wine wasabi jus in a separate pouring jug.

Makes 1 bowl (the sauce will be enough for 4 portions)

inari sushi stuffed with kinpira burdock & carrot

see variations page 272

Inari is made from deep-fried tofu, or abura-age, which is cut into thin slices, press-drained, and deep-fried again.

1/2 burdock root
1 tsp. rice vinegar and a bowl of ice water
1 carrot
2 tsp. white sesame seeds
1/2 tbsp. mirin
2 tbsp. soy sauce

3 tbsp. dashi (page 44)
1 red chile
1 tbsp. toasted sesame oil
2 1/2 tbsp. shari rice (page 28)
2 inari pouches, washed (purchased as they are from a Japanese grocery)

Burdock comes as a long muddy root. Scrub (rather than peel) the outside well to remove the dirt and lightly scrape off the skin with a knife. Burdock is a very healthy root and much of the nutrient and flavor content lies just under the skin, so try to preserve it. Cut into thin julienned strips about 1-in. long. Once cut, place the strips into a bowl of cold water with a teaspoon of rice vinegar in it to prevent them from discoloring. After peeling the carrot, cut it into similar julienned strips. Roast the sesame seeds in a dry pan. Combine the mirin, soy, and dashi in a bowl. Finely chop the chile. Strain and dry the burdock. In a frying pan heat the sesame oil and add the burdock and carrot. Sauté over medium heat until slightly softened. Then add the mirin, soy, and dashi and simmer gently with the lid off for 5–10 minutes until the liquid is mostly absorbed. Take it off the heat and stir in the chile and toasted sesame seeds. Mix this "kinpira" mixture with the shari rice. Stuff the prepared inari with the shari rice and kinpira mixture. Fold the inari into a small neat parcel.
Makes 3 inari

inari sushi stuffed with edamame soybean & jamón

see variations page 273

The little stuffed tofu pouches also lend themselves to less traditional combinations. Here we take inspiration from the classic Spanish tapas dish habas con jamón, beans with ham.

10 edamame beans, boiled
3/4 oz. serrano or iberico ham
2 1/2 tbsp. shari rice (page 28)

2 inari pouches, washed (purchased as they are from a Japanese grocery)
black pepper

Edamame beans can usually be found in the freezer section of a grocery store, and come ready shelled, like peas. Boil the edamame beans briefly, so that they remain firm.

Chop the ham into small pieces and mix into the shari rice with the boiled edamame. Season with black pepper. Stuff the prepared inari with the ham, rice, and edamame mixture. Fold the inari into a small neat parcel.

Makes 3 inari

onigiri rice balls &
oven-poached salmon

see variations page 274

Rice is of extraordinary importance in Japanese culture, and no more so as when used in the humble rice ball onigiri, which is considered a meal in itself.

3 1/2 oz. salmon fillet
1 cup soy
1/2 cup rice vinegar
1/2 cup mirin

1 1/4 cups boiled white short-grain rice
2 nori sheets
sea salt

A plastic onigiri mold helps if you have one, but it isn't necessary.

Place the salmon in a small ovenproof dish. Combine the soy, vinegar, and mirin and pour over the salmon. Poach in an oven preheated to 350°F for about 10–15 minutes, depending on the thickness of your fillet. When cool, shred into small pieces. Stir in the cooked rice with a pinch of salt. Mix the rice and the shredded salmon together. Take a large handful (3 oz.) of the salmon-rice in your hand and press until it doesn't fall apart. Make a spherical shape first, then gently press between your palms to create a more triangular shape. That will slightly flatten the ball. Cut a sheet of nori into a long length of the same width as your onigiri. Wrap the onigiri as shown in the picture on page 274. If you live near a Japanese grocery, you may find this style of elaborate wrapping there. It's designed especially so the nori won't get soggy!

Makes 4 onigiri

picnic-wrapped tuna salad onigiri

see variations page 275

A more homely style of onigiri is to partially wrap it in nori, making it yet more portable – this style is often chosen for picnics. From a Japanese viewpoint, there is something very comforting about this style of onigiri; it is just as your mom might have made for your school lunch box.

5 oz. canned tuna in water
4 tsp. finely chopped onion
12 oz. boiled white short-grain rice

1 nori sheet
white sesame seeds

A plastic onigiri mold helps if you have one, but it isn't necessary.

Drain the canned tuna and combine with the chopped onion.

Take a large handful (3 oz.) of rice in your hand, and press until it doesn't fall apart. Make a spherical shape and then make a small indentation in one side. Spoon into the hollow a teaspoon of tuna–onion mix. Press the rice together to conceal it. Once you have the spherical shape again, gently press between your palms to create a more triangular shape, slightly flattening the ball.

Cut a sheet of nori into 4 pieces. Wrap a piece of it around the center of the onigiri as shown in the picture on page 275. Sprinkle with sesame seeds.

Makes 4 onigiri

yaki-broiled rice balls onigiri

see variations page 276

The broiled rice ball is another popular version of the humble onigiri, often found in local pub-style izakayas, and usually served with pickles.

12 oz. boiled short-grain rice
4 tsp. soy sauce
pickles

Make the onigiri rice ball shape as described in the recipe on page 256.

Broil on each side for about 2 minutes. Brush with a teaspoon of soy sauce and place under the broiler again just to toast off. Be wary of adding too much soy, as this will break up the rice.

Serve with a bowl of miso soup, oshinko pickles, or cucumber pickles.

Makes 4 onigiri

classic japanese vegetables in onigiri rice balls

see variations page 277

Furthering the notion of the onigiri being the perfect snack food for its portability and ease of making, using traditional Japanese vegetable ingredients also helps prolong its shelf life on picnics or packed lunches.

3 tbsp. hijiki seaweed
soy sauce
12 oz. boiled white short-grain rice

1 nori sheet
black sesame seeds

Hijiki is a type of dark brown seaweed that looks like small twigs. It is high in calcium and contains plenty of fiber. Hijiki seaweed can be purchased at a Japanese grocery in its dry form, so you will need to rehydrate it in water for 30 minutes or so. Once softened, drain and mix with a dash of soy sauce.

Make the onigiri rice ball shape as described in the base recipe (page 256), placing the hijiki in the small hollow.

Cut a sheet of nori into 4 pieces. Wrap a piece around the center of the onigiri as shown in the picture opposite. Sprinkle with black sesame seed.

Makes 4 onigiri

cabbage parcels, tamago, rice & peas

see variations page 278

This is a delightful little addition to any picnic, and it's not as hard as it looks!

4 large savoy cabbage leaves
ice water
1 1/2 oz. tamago omelet (page 189)
mitsuba leaves or chives

2 3/4 oz. shari rice (page 28)
1 tbsp. peas, blanched
toasted black sesame seeds
toothpicks

Cut out the hard stem at the base of the cabbage. Blanch the cabbage leaves in a large saucepan of boiling water for a minute. Remove and immediately plunge into ice water, preventing the leaves from losing their color.

Dice the tamago omelet. Chop the mitsuba leaves and mix with the shari rice, peas, tamago, and sesame seed.

Place one cabbage leaf on a chopping board and spoon on top a quarter of the rice mixture. Fold over the bottom and top of the cabbage leaf and then the sides, making a neat parcel. Secure it with a toothpick.

Makes 4 cabbage parcels

oshi zushi pressed sushi ham & cheese

see variations page 279

Pressed sushi is the oldest form of sushi and was first used as a means of preserving fish by packing it tightly in a box of fermenting rice. In the earliest forms of sushi, only the preserved fish was eaten and the rice was actually discarded.

2 3/4 oz. cured ham, sliced very thinly
3/4 oz. iceberg lettuce leaves, uncut
2 3/4 oz. Gruyère (or any hard cheese of your
    choice), cut into very thin slices

Japanese mustard
1/2 cup shari rice (page 28)

Traditionally, this is made using a wooden mold, but if you don't have one, then use an oblong cake loaf pan with sides as straight as possible! The traditional size of a mold is 6 x 3 in. If you are using a loaf pan, line it with plastic wrap. If you are using a wooden mold, soak it in water to prevent the rice from sticking. Arrange the ham in layers at the bottom of the container. Add a layer of iceberg leaves. Top with a layer of Gruyère and smear a little mustard over the cheese (as desired). Add the shari rice to the mold or loaf pan, and use your fingers to pack down the rice. Put the lid on the mold and press it down to compact the rice. Remove the sides of the mold by pressing on the lid, then take the lid off and carefully turn the mold over and eject the block onto a chopping board, with the ham side now facing up. To make it more decorative, you can arrange the ingredients with diagonal slices of hard cheese placed first, as shown in the picture. Wrap in plastic wrap and store in a cool place (ideally not as cool as a refrigerator) for up to 5 hours. When ready to use, dip a sharp knife in water and cut the block into 6 equal pieces.

Makes 6 pieces

oshi zushi pressed sushi with atsu-age deep-fried tofu

see variations page 280

When I first went to Japan, the slightly grubby station kiosks were always full of forsaken-looking boxes of pressed mackerel sushi. Nowadays, oshi zushi is little seen other than the infrequent packed lunch for school, though the nostalgia lingers at railway bento-box kiosks, where the traditional version of vinegared mackerel is always something to pick up for a train trip back to your hometown.

3 1/2 oz. atsu-age dried and fried tofu
4 tsp. pickled cucumber (page 49)
1/2 avocado

wasabi
1/2 cup shari rice (page 28)
1 nori sheet cut to size of container

Atsu-age or abura-age (a smaller version of it) can be found in Japanese groceries and should be rinsed in hot water to remove the excess oil. Cut into 1/3-in. thick slices and line the bottom of a mold with it, making sure there are no gaps. Cut the pickled cucumber into long, thin slices and lay over the abura-age. Roughly chop the avocado and layer on top of the cucumber. Smear with wasabi to taste.

Fill the rice half way and pack down, then place the cut piece of nori on top of the rice. Add the remainder of the rice and pack down. Continue making the oshi zushi as described in the previous recipe (page 265).

Makes 6 pieces

halloumi cheese & greek salad rice bowl with yuzu vinaigrette

see variations page 281

A quick, healthy, and easy light lunch; essentially a rice salad with endless possibilities to use your favorite vegetables and cheese.

soy sauce, for glazing
1 oz. diced halloumi cheese
1 oz. diced avocado
1 oz. diced red pepper
1 oz. diced cherry tomato
1 oz. diced cucumber
1/2 tsp. mizuna

1/2 oz. black olives, pitted and halved
1 1/2 cups shari rice (page 28)
sea salt & black pepper
sesame seeds
nori, to garnish
2 tsp. yuzu vinaigrette (page 52)

Brush a little soy sauce over the halloumi cheese and broil on each side for a minute or so until golden on each side. Gently mix all the diced vegetables and mizuna together with the halloumi and arrange on top of a bowl of warm shari rice, reserving a few black olives for decoration. Sprinkle with salt, pepper and sesame seeds, garnish with the olives and strips of cut nori, and serve with a yuzu vinaigrette.

It is also nice to serve this dish with the rice mixed gently in with the chopped vegetables, creating a shari rice salad. Brown rice is of course also lovely to use here.

Makes 1 portion

chirashi of shiitake mushroom, lotus root & bamboo

see base recipe page 247

tamago omelet, ham & shishito peppers chirashi
Prepare the basic recipe, replacing vegetables with 2 shredded shishito peppers and 1 oz. tamago omelet. Replace tofu with 1 1/2 oz. ham, cut into 1/3-in. cubes. Sprinkle with nori to serve.

ume plum & shiso chirashi
Prepare the basic recipe, replacing vegetables with 3–4 whole umeboshi plums, omitting marinade and tofu. Tear 2 shiso leaves and mix with 1 tablespoon ume plum paste. Sprinkle over plums, with sesame seeds and nori on top.

edamame, soybean & jamón chirashi
Prepare the basic recipe, replacing vegetables with 1 oz. steamed soybeans and tofu with 1 1/2 oz. jamón, cut into cubes. Scatter on top with the soybeans, tamago, and nori.

kinpira burdock & carrot chirashi
Omit vegetables, marinade, omelet, and tofu. Prepare burdock root and carrot as described on page 252. Top with sesame seeds, chopped scallions, and shredded nori.

tororo mountain yam potato and tuna chirashi
Omit vegetables, marinade, omelet, and tofu. Grate 1 3/4 oz. Japanese mountain yam, or nagaimo, chop marinated cubes of tuna (page 58), and serve sprinkled with chopped scallion.

classic chirashi scattered fish

see base recipe page 248

aji no tataki chopped horse mackerel & scallion chirashi
Prepare the basic recipe, replacing fish with 2 3/4 oz. horse mackerel as prepared on page 94.
Mix with 1 oz. chopped scallion and 2 teaspoons ponzu sauce and decorate with wasabi and
long pieces of chives.

negitoro "belly of tuna" and scallion chirashi
Prepare the basic receipe, replacing fish with tuna prepared as described on page 222.
Arrange on top of 1 oz. chopped scallion and 1/2 oz. shredded iceberg lettuce. Decorate with
wasabi and long pieces of chives.

scallop & ikura salmon roe chirashi
Prepare the basic recipe, replacing fish with 2 large scallops as prepared on page 110 and cut
into cubes. Julienne about 1 oz. cucumber. Place the scallops over the cucumber, top with
2 teaspoons salmon roe, and decorate with shiso cress.

unagi "faux eel" kabayaki chirashi
Prepare the basic receipe, replacing fish with faux eel as prepared on page 222. Top with
shichimi pepper and some pickles on the side, as you like.

salmon ju
Prepare the basic receipe, replacing fish with slices of salmon sashimi. Serve covering a bed
of rice topped with a dab of wasabi and a teaspoon of salmon roe.

seared beef chirashi with red wine & wasabi jus

see base recipe page 251

seared duck with umeshu plum wine & wasabi jus chirashi
Prepare the basic recipe, replacing beef with duck, searing skin-side down first, omitting butter when frying. Replace mirin and red wine with 6 tablespoons of plum wine.

seared chicken with sake & wasabi jus chirashi
Prepare the basic recipe, replacing beef with chicken breast, searing skin-side down first, but cook the chicken longer so as to cook through the center. Replace mirin and red wine with 6 tablespoons of sake.

seared quail with red wine & wasabi jus chirashi
Prepare the basic recipe, replacing beef with quail breast, searing skin-side down first and frying for a slightly shorter time.

seared venison with umeshu plum wine & wasabi jus chirashi
Prepare the basic recipe, replacing beef with venison. Replace mirin and red wine with 6 tablespoons of plum wine.

variations

inari sushi stuffed with kinpira burdock & carrot

see base recipe page 252

spinach & sesame inari

Omit burdock and carrot. Blanch a few spinach leaves 20 seconds and drain. Toast
1 teaspoon white sesame seeds in a dry heavy-bottomed pan and then grind them in a
mortar. Prepare a mixture of soy sauce with your choice of apple juice, sugar, or mirin. Add
the ground sesame seeds and mix well. Add spinach, mix with the rice, and stuff the inari.

tamago omelet & Japanese mushrooms inari

Prepare the basic recipe, replacing burdock and carrot with a selection of shiitake, enoki, or
nameko mushrooms. Mix with shreds of omelet before stuffing.

ginko nut & shiso inari

Prepare the basic recipe, replacing burdock and carrot with 10 whole, ready prepared ginko
nuts from a Japanese grocery, crushed. Mix with 2 torn shiso leaves before stuffing.

renkon lotus root & nira garlic shoots inari

Prepare the basic recipe, replacing burdock and carrot with equal quantities of renkon and
garlic shoots, prepared in the kinpira style.

pickled ginger, kanpyo calabash gourd strips & carrot inari

Prepare the basic recipe, replacing burdock and carrot with calabash strips and carrot
prepared in the kinpira style. Mix with a little chopped pickled ginger before stuffing.

inari sushi stuffed with edamame soybean & jamón

see base recipe page 255

octopus & pea inari
Prepare the basic recipe, replacing jamón with octopus as prepared on page 74 and replacing edamame with boiled green peas.

tataki beef inari
Prepare the basic recipe, replacing jamón with beef as prepared on page 77, chopped into small pieces. Omit edamame.

halloumi & sunblush tomato inari
Prepare the basic recipe, replacing jamón with 1 oz. halloumi cheese, toasted and cut into chunks. Replace edamame with 2 tablespoons chopped sunblush tomato.

simmered pumpkin & walnut inari
Prepare the basic recipe, replacing jamón with nimono-style simmered pumpkin as described on page 73, chopped into small chunks. Replace edamame with walnuts, toasted in a dry pan and then crushed.

mentaiko chili pollock roe & lime inari
Prepare the basic recipe, replacing jamón and edamame with 1 oz. mentaiko chili pollock roe (available from Japanese grocery stores). Mix into shari rice with a little lime zest.

variations

onigiri rice balls & oven-poached salmon

see base recipe page 256

tuna kakuni with soy ginger onigiri
Prepare the basic recipe, replacing salmon with tuna, poached with one teaspoon of grated ginger.

poached tuna with shichimi onigiri
Prepare the basic recipe, replacing salmon with tuna, poached with a sprinkle of shichimi pepper.

poached salmon with yuzukosho onigiri
Prepare the basic recipe. When the poached salmon is cool, shred it and mix in 1/2 teaspoon of yuzukosho paste.

furikake onigiri
Prepare the basic recipe, replacing salt with furikake (a rice seasoning available at most Japanese grocery stores, containing sesame seeds, wasabi powder, and other spices such as sansho pepper). Omit salmon.

picnic-wrapped tuna salad onigiri

see base recipe page 257

katsuo boshi bonito flakes onigiri
Prepare the basic recipe, omitting tuna. Fill the hollow with some bonito flakes and a tiny dash of soy.

sunblush tomato, scallion & mozzarella onigiri
Prepare the basic recipe, omitting tuna. Finely chop 4 sunblush tomatoes, 4 teaspoons scallion, and 3/4 oz. mozzarella and spoon into the hollow.

tuna salad & corn onigiri
Prepare the basic recipe, adding 2 oz. corn to the tuna before filling the hollow.

tuna salad & jalepeño onigiri
Prepare the basic recipe, adding 1 oz. of finely chopped jalepeño to the tuna before filling the hollow.

variations

yaki-broiled rice balls onigiri

see base recipe page 259

genmai brown rice yaki onigiri
Prepare the basic recipe, replacing rice with genmai brown rice (page 47).

teriyaki-glazed yaki onigiri
Prepare the basic recipe, replacing soy sauce with teriyaki sauce (page 36).

bacon & mozzarella yaki onigiri
Prepare the basic recipe. Broil one side first, then top the second side of each onigiri with a very thin slice of mozzarella and 1/2 a strip of bacon. Broil until bacon is cooked through.

cheese & green pepper yaki onigiri
Prepare the basic recipe. Broil on one side first, then top the second side with a hard cheese such as Gruyère. Sprinkle chopped green pepper on top and broil until the cheese has melted.

oshinko pickle yaki onigiri
Prepare the basic recipe, placing a round slice of oshinko pickled daikon radish on top, just before the soy sauce is brushed on.

bamboo shoot yaki onigiri
Prepare the basic recipe, topping one side with a slice of boiled bamboo just before the soy sauce is brushed on.

variations

classic japanese vegetables in onigiri rice balls

see base recipe page 260

natto fermented soybean & scallion onigiri
Prepare the basic recipe, replacing seaweed with 3/4 oz. chopped scallion mixed with
3/4 oz. natto.

pickled cucumber onigiri
Prepare the basic recipe, replacing seaweed with chopped pickled cucumber as prepared in
on page 49.

ume plum & shiso onigiri
Prepare the basic recipe, replacing seaweed with 4 whole umeboshi plums mixed with
2 chopped shiso leaves.

moromiso & scallion onigiri
Prepare the basic recipe, replacing seaweed with 3/4 oz. moromiso paste mixed with
3/4 oz. chopped scallion.

variations

cabbage parcels, tamago, rice & peas

see base recipe page 262

tamago omelet, pea & gomoku brown rice cabbage parcel
Prepare the basic recipe, replacing rice with 5-grain rice (page 47).

edamame & ham cabbage parcel
Prepare the basic recipe, replacing the peas with boiled edamame and replacing the tamago with small pieces of ham. Season with Japanese mustard.

halloumi cheese & sunblush tomato cabbage parcel
Prepare the basic recipe, replacing the tamago with 1 1/2 oz. halloumi, toasted and cut into small chunks. Omit peas and mix rice with 4 chopped sunblush tomatoes.

edamame & chorizo cabbage parcel
Prepare the basic recipe, replacing the peas with boiled edamame and replacing the tamago with small pieces of chorizo. Season with smoked paprika mayonnaise (page 50).

halloumi cheese & olive cabbage parcel
Prepare the basic recipe, replacing the tamago with 1 1/2 oz. halloumi, toasted and cut into small chunks. Omit peas and mix rice with 6 chopped green or black olives.

variations

oshi zushi pressed sushi ham & cheese

see base recipe page 265

bamboo shoot & pine nut pressed sushi
Prepare the basic recipe, replacing ham and cheese with 3 oz. bamboo shoot and
4 teaspoons pine nuts. Using canned or vacuum-packed bamboo, simmer as on page 73. Cut
into thin slices and sprinkle with pine nuts before pressing down the rice.

tataki seared beef & shiso cress pressed sushi
Prepare the basic recipe, replacing ham and cheese with beef and cress. Sprinkle shiso cress
on the bottom of the mold. Prepare the tataki beef as described on page 77, place the beef
on top of the shiso cress and smear with a bit of wasabi or Japanese mustard.

avocado & smoked paprika mayonnaise pressed sushi
Prepare the basic recipe, omitting ham and cheese. Line the mold with 1/2 large avocado, cut
into slices, and smear with a little smoked paprika mayonnaise (page 50).

yuba soy milk skin & wasabi pressed sushi
Prepare the basic recipe, replacing ham and cheese with 4 slices yuba (which can be
purchased pre-sliced in a specialist Japanese grocery) and smear with a little wasabi.

variations

oshi zushi pressed sushi with atsu-age deep-fried tofu

see base recipe page 266

vinegared mackerel pressed sushi
Prepare the basic recipe, replacing atsu-age with vinegared mackerel as prepared on page 61, and lay the slices across the base of the mold. Smear with a little wasabi.

shrimp pressed sushi
Prepare the basic recipe, replacing atsu-age with shrimp as prepared on page 225. Line the mold with the shrimp, top side down, and add wasabi as desired.

faux eel unagi pressed sushi
Prepare the basic recipe, replacing atsu-age with faux unagi eel as prepared on page 222. Line the mold with the faux eel, basting with a little of the sauce.

lemon sole, shiso pressed sushi
Prepare the basic recipe, replacing atsu-age with a fillet of sole, cut to size, and line the mold. Place the shiso leaf on the sole. The pressed result when turned out of the mold shows the green of the shiso shining through the translucence of the sole flesh.

tamago omelet pressed sushi
Prepare the basic recipe, replacing atsu-age with a 1/3-in.-thick piece of omelet placed at the bottom of the mold.

variations

halloumi cheese & greek salad rice bowl with yuzu vinaigrette

see base recipe page 268

tamago omelet, ham & shishito peppers rice bowl
Prepare the basic recipe, omitting cheese and olives. Cut 2 oz. organic ham into 1/2-in. cubes, scatter on top of the rice with shreds of omelet. Salt and gently broil 2 shishito peppers, deeseeded and sliced. Arrange on the rice and sprinkle with shreds of nori.

ume plum & shiso rice bowl
This is a classic combination, and as the ume plums are so tart, you won't need to cover the whole surface of the bowl. Tear some leaves of shiso and mix with the puree of 4 whole umeboshi plums, sprinkle sesame seeds and nori on top.

edamame, soybean & jamon rice bowl
Prepare the basic recipe, omitting cheese and olives. Cut 2 oz. Spanish style ham into cubes, steam 2 tablespoons soybeans, and scatter on top with shreds of tamago omelet and nori.

index